the Authentic Self

~

Brian C. Taylor

the Authentic Self
by Brian C. Taylor
Published by Postpaper / Lulu
ISBN 978-1-304-28652-9

Printed on demand to save paper
First printing October 2013
Copyright 2010 Brian C. Taylor / Postpaper / Lulu
As originally published in:
Anti-Social Engineering the Hyper-Manipulated Self
excluding introduction and edits.

Please visit http://www.anti-socialengineering.com

Table of Contents

1
Introduction

When I first began working on the problem of Authenticity in 2006, it was a direct response to the success of people like Eckhart Tolle and Dr. Phil. These men, and others like them, were talking about "the Authentic Self" as if it we're obtainable by understanding what was lacking in your life. Mr. Tolle, author of "self help" books said he was spurred into the pursuit of authenticity by discovering he was "disappointed with himself." Tolle thought there was something to be learned in the tiny phrase: "I am (whatever adjective) with my self," and asked "Who is the I and who is the self?" Obviously he was not the first person to have such thoughts, which can be traced back most notably to Aristotle. Mr. Tolle then went on to write two terrible books that make absolutely no sense. If it wasn't for Oprah Winfrey liking his books, no one would have ever had to waste their time.

Dr. Phil, on the other hand, a trained counsellor, also made famous by Oprah, strangely kept referring to the Authentic Self as a product of you living up to God's plan for yourself. I don't have anything against psychology, or God for that matter, but I do find it odd that a man who claims to be a scientist would choose the most unscientific methods in an attempt to help people discover who they actually are and how they got that way. Dr. Phil might bring into it past events that helped form the memories, experiences and events that shaped your personality and any faults you might have with it, but he does not go far enough into our beings as a product of modernity.

By the time I had published *Anti-Social Engineering the Hyper-Manipulated Self,* which took four years of writing and study I had accomplished what I set out to do: Define a pathway to a true scientific understanding of what the Authentic Self is, how to uncover it, how to achieve it and how to maintain it. Readers may enjoy the fruit of my labour by purchase that book or reading blog entries from my website, but this new collection you hold in your hands is the nuts and bolts of Authenticity. As such, it will be quite dry to most and certainly lacking the false comfort provided by Mr. Tolle or Dr. Phil. It is, however, thorough in its details and mathematically precise in its philosophy. It is nothing short of the most accurate understanding of the Authentic Self currently available.

This book, like most of my writing, is written like an entire scholastic career. This is meant to ease you into the basics of what become extremely complicated matters of philosophy, psychology and sociology. Think of it as starting at Kindergarten and eventually getting your Doctorate, in Authenticity. For example, when you are a child you are, (hopefully) sent to school to learn your ABC's. As you work your way through elementary school, you continue to hone your mastery of the ABCs into spelling, grammar, vocabulary, etc. When you get into high school you begin to have an appreciation of the power of the words you can now build out of your initial understanding of the ABCs, into, for instance, Shakespeare. Until ultimately, if you are so inclined, you might go to college to learn how to "be a Shakespeare" yourself. So where once you didn't know what those squiggly shapes were, you now may use those shapes forming words, sentences, ideas, knowledge and understanding. Doing philosophy by way of symbolic logic is not dissimilar to the analogy and we will be required to use some as we work through this book.

Thus, in the first three chapters we will dip our toes in, explain some of the methodology of doing simple logic problems and set our definitions. Then we will wade into a real understanding of what those definitions are and what their relationships to each other mean. Finally, we will attempt to attach meaningful purpose to our beings by way of a true, scientific understanding of how we became who we are.

All of our work begins and ends with the chart on the next page, which I call the Philosophy Generator.

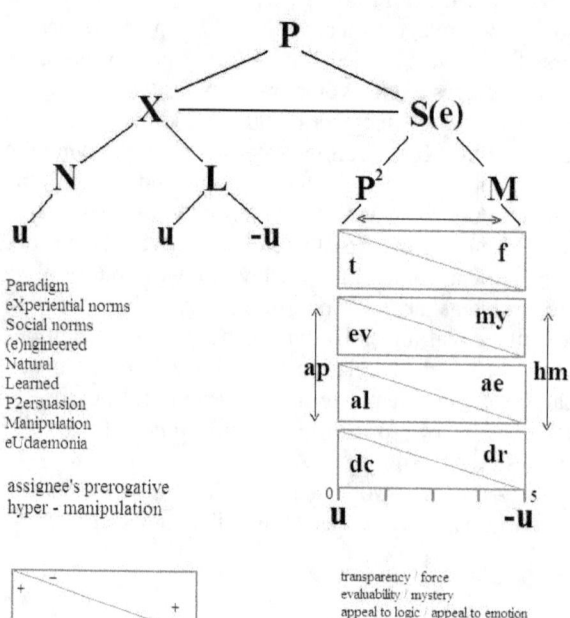

Paradigm
eXperiential norms
Social norms
(e)ngineered
Natural
Learned
P2ersuasion
Manipulation
eUdaemonia

assignee's prerogative
hyper - manipulation

transparency / force
evaluability / mystery
appeal to logic / appeal to emotion
desire to concur / desire to resist

2
the Philosophy Generator

Imagine, in your brain, there is a complicated network of associations. Every single thought you have comes from some combination of these associations. It is these associations that are the concern of the Philosophy Generator, (the chart,) and this is what we must now address.

P is for **paradigm**. A paradigm is a grouping of associations you have on any subject. Associations are any thought, memory, feeling, or idea and a grouping of them creates a mental model or conceptualization. No matter how many associations from which you construct a subjects' paradigm there is only one paradigm per subject. With P at the top of the Philosophy Generator it is the culmination of our concern and everything underneath it must be a constituent of that paradigm. For illustrative purposes, we will consider your "Fire Paradigm." I have chosen "fire" because it is a universal paradigm that everyone can relate to, have experiences with and comprehend. Any and all associations you might have about "fire" are included, whether you're aware of them or not. ("Fire" is a concrete example, but all ideas, even abstract ideas like "love" or "the colour red" are arranged in paradigm.) I'm sure you can think of a long list of "fire" associations. Typical examples might include: fire is hot, fire burns, fire hurts, fire is useful (for heat, light, warmth, cooking,) fire can kill, fire can cleanse my spirit, fire is portable, fire is symbolic, fire can destroy, fire can cauterize, fire can power my steam engine, fire can propel us into space, fire will appease the Gods...

X is for **experiential norm**. An experiential norm is an association you have constructed through your own experience. Obviously, every association one makes is a personal experience and my associations, on even the same subjects, will be different from yours. Such sentences must be considered in their entirety as not just statements, but complete and total ideas, as per the rules of Philosophy. So when it is said that, "An experiential norm is an association you have constructed through your own experience," it is meant that it is only this and cannot be anything else. In other words, an experiential norm is an association that you have made without the influences of other peoples' associations. It is what you have come up with, when left to your own devices.

Looking at our list of associations for our "Fire Paradigm" we can now pick out the ones that are experiential norms: fire is hot, fire burns, fire hurts, fire can destroy, etc... It should be noted that any of these associations could have been taught to you, such as your mother may have taught you that the "oven" is "hot" and "mustn't be touched." (Thus, three associations join to create the Paradigm, "Hot ovens mustn't be touched.") If this was the case, then in fairness to our definitions, these examples would not qualify as experiential, until you had actually experienced the pain caused by touching a hot oven. Thus, these examples are common, and fair use, as sooner or later in this life, despite being taught, everyone burns themselves and sees something destroyed by fire.

In philosophical terms, experiential norms are knowledge by acquaintance. Knowledge by acquaintance is empirical, (verifiable by observation or experience, not reliant on theory or pure logic.) You know something to be factual because you've had personal experience with it. You are acquainted with a paradigm when it is determined by sense data, (information received by the five senses.) Such is it that a human may easily, through X, learn that fire burns.

S is for **Social Norm**. "Social norm" is a term borrowed from Sociology and in our context, it changes very little. A social norm is an association that you have constructed entirely from influence(s) or are the paradigm of an individual or group, other than you. These are the associations you have not made for yourself, they are not "your own devices." In philosophical terms a social norm is knowledge by description. This means that you have learned of this association from sources outside your own experiences via their "description." (Which could be a lesson, demonstration, story, the point is you are not directly sensing the associative data yourself, it is "second hand.") It is possible for a social norm to become an experiential norm via "acquaintance" or having been personally experienced. This is why the Philosophy Generator has a line under P connecting S to X. It is a completely reasonable thing to say both that that an experience can be taught and a lesson can be experienced.

(Such as your Mother taught you the oven is hot, but odds are, you're going to burn yourself at some point.) Later we will examine what it means when a social norm cannot be experienced. These types of associations, the kind that can't be directly experienced, we will refer to as "strict." Looking at our list of "fire associations," we can now pick out those that strictly fall into the category of social norms: "Fire will appease the Gods." "Fire can cleanse my spirit."

There is no rule that states that any particular Paradigm has to be either X or S. It must be at least one, but it can be built from associations that come from both experiential and social norms. Such is the case with certain aspects of our "fire" paradigm. Let's examine the practice of cauterization with a hot iron. At some point in history an ancestor of ours, already having carried fire into the iron age, learning from elders who have passed down "the knowledge" of fire's utility, somehow discovered that holding a red hot iron to flesh would "melt it together," closing a wound. For that person, this realization was an experiential norm developed from previous social norms and one experience. (Some individual would have to have "done it first," possibly thousands of years previous, with a burning ember, held in moss. This matters not for we are discussing the paradigm of cauterization with a hot iron.) Thus, the paradigm has associations of lesson: Fire, heat, iron work, and finally, perhaps by accident, the experience of cauterization was discovered. For everyone that he taught this to and then for everyone they taught this to, cauterization would be a social norm. For you, it would stay "S" until you "X'd" it. (Again, you don't have to be the one being cauterized to have this experience, you could just as readily see it happen.) If the associations of a particular paradigm come from both sides of the Philosophy Generator they are said to have a "mixed constituency."

So far, we have examined what constitutes a particular paradigm, "fire," and where those constituents originated, either X and/or S. Now we must look at how we first experienced these associations. Did we learn them? Were they the product of instinct and common sense or expectation due to existence?

L is for **Learned**. These are the associations that had to have been created anew. There are three types of learned associations and each of this has a place in the Philosophy Generator. "What? There aren't three L positions in the PG!" In the philosophy generator, and in life, there are strict social norms that must be learned, shared, passed between people. Remember, because it is strict it cannot be X, cannot be experienced. Call them SL. This may mean that you were instructed by another, for instance, in the task of burning an effigy. It could even be that you have no particular feelings toward the target of your symbolic sacrifice. You have simply been told who to hate and believed it. It has not been your experience that the effigy deserves to be a target, nor do you feel appropriately hostile. You are a product of only influence. So is the strictness defined.

The second L position belongs to X, attached to S. Call it SXL. These are learned social norms that can be experienced. It could mean that you were taught something like cauterization or just observed people walk on hot coals without hurting their feet. In this instance you are not being taught, but you are still learning from another, therefore either of these learned association is a social norm.

Anything you have learned, independent of others' paradigm, completely on your own is a strict learned experiential norm. This third and final L in the philosophy generator defines the lessons we learn on our own. Often these are the lessons we remember the best, having lived the experience.

N is for a **Naturally occurring** experiential norms. These are the associations we find necessary, unavoidable and inevitable. We are born with these paradigm, or they become exemplary, (required) . These are the types of things that we don't even think about, they just are. We don't have to be instructed to hold our breath underwater, we come equipped to understand that fire will hurt us if we let it, we experience love for our children, all without needing to be instructed how.

Perhaps, by now, you have calculated why it is that there is no N under S. If an association is a social norm it is because it has come from influence. A naturally occurring experiential norm, by definition, must be universally experienced. Strict social norms, (those that can't be experienced,) can never be considered Natural. It is possible for a social norm to become N if it can be X'd, Then, as a product of experiential norms, the association can no longer be S. This can get confusing and we will go into greater detail later. For now, consider the easiest example, "love." Love is a powerful emotion that is a

Brian C. Taylor

experience you must feel personally. However, you must have someone or something to love, so it seems like it should be a social norm. This is because you are confusing what it is the Philosophy Generator measures. We are not determining what is required for you to feel love, (you, someone else and a connection, presumably.) We are seeking what you think about love, how you think about love and from where did these ideas originate. Don't let the universality of the Generator muddy the waters, we are only concerned with the constituents of paradigm.

The final term in the Philosophy Generator is U. **U** stands for **Eudaemonia**. I've chosen U over E, because E is used elsewhere and the word is pronounced, "You-de-mon-ee-ah." Eudaemonia is an ancient Greek word that was developed into a philosophy of "happiness" by Aristotle. This, like all of the concepts being introduced here, will be examined to their ends, soon enough. All you need to understand at this point is that there are associations you will determine to be useful or appropriate, in addition to the ones you feel are counterproductive. Eudaemonics will be what we use to determine this qualification. The definition of eudaemonia has wandered over the last 2400 years but in the shortest terms and the lowest common denominators, it is some combination of altruism and selfishness. Aristotle's happiness was not only a product of his desires, but also the promotion of what he determined to be good, so it is that he could feel content in his person, social network, city, nation, species and world, knowing he has done well by his turn at existence.

the Authentic Self

Where the Philosophy Generator is the means, Assignee's Prerogative is the ends. This is the discerning of your "Authentic Self." Assignee's prerogative states that you give the paradigms you have their weight, worth, value, power and strength. It is the Atheists' prerogative to assign little power to his "God paradigm." It is the Preachers' prerogative to do the opposite. Those of us who waltz through life unaware of the amazing intricacies of the human psyche will have no use for understanding Assignee's Prerogative. These people will still be assigning worth to their paradigms but without contemplating them will have no means to achieve any sort of awareness. Conversely, once we have been made aware of Assignee's Prerogative we must accept responsibility and be accountable to our consciousness. Thus, enlightenment is not a frivolous pursuit.

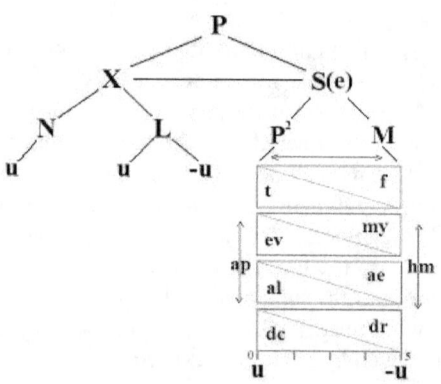

3
Defining the Constituents
of Paradigm

At the top of the generator is Paradigm. This is divided into two possible sources: eXperiential and Social, the differences of these must be fully understood before we can continue. An experience is something that only you can have. That is not to say that only you can have one but rather that only you can have yours. An experience, essentially, is data recognition. Information goes into your nervous system through your five senses and is processed into an experience. There are no experiences to be had without information. Even two experiencers processing "the same data" will do so differently. What is information? It's easier to answer than you might think. Everything is information. Granted, this three word sentence deserves probably an entire tome to itself. We don't need to examine how everything is information to gain the insight we seek. We also needn't concern ourselves with a computers' ability to process information to understand that there is a difference between it and what we are capable of. Truth be known, a coffee table is having the experience of a being a coffee table. It is chock full of "coffee table information," right down to the molecular level. We can see, feel, smell and even taste the table if we require some data from it. We cannot be the table any more than we can ask the computer what being a table is like.

These are the conundrums of philosophy and they can be pushed to the utmost. (What is a thing anyway? An object? Anything? There are things. Things exist. There are not things that don't exist. Is "love" a thing as much as a "table" is? It seems ridiculous to even want to contemplate such statements, yet here we are...) If you find yourself inclined to wonder about such things it is entirely possible that you have already asked yourself whether or not I am referring to paradigms themselves, or the ideas that the paradigms represent? This ages old question was named by Immanuel Kant as "The phenomenon of the thing vs. the thing itself." Kant explained that we can't get to know the thing itself because we "get in the things' way" by sensing it. The "thing," in actuality is a product of the "thing" and our perception of it. For our purposes, despite the apparent importance, this question is irrelevant. We can consider both the ideas of our paradigms, (the associations,) and the paradigms themselves, (the combination of associations,) separately or together. For instance, it's likely that no one would waste any time arguing that knowing fire spreads and destroys was problematic, but they might argue against the merits of arson. The difference being that a piece of your "fire" paradigm, while actually attached in some way to your "arson" paradigm, it is not representative of your complete thoughts on either subject.

Brian C. Taylor

Bertrand Russell commented on Plato's thoughts on this subject as well. Using the terms I have chosen, Russell says that any association is a "Particular" and any paradigm is a "Universal" built out of "particulars." He goes on to differentiate these as "the characteristics of" and just "of." For example: "A just act" or "a red thing" versus "Justice" or "Redness." Physicists too talk about the phenomenon of observational interference right down to the subatomic level. Suffice to say, I don't think we'll be breaking any new ground here today. Just know that, in terms of paradigm, the thing *is* the idea and vice versa.

So let us end our questions of experience with the following: "An experience is YOU, processing data. That is all." We, unlike a coffee table, are able to think about that process but that doesn't make the coffee table experience any less real. The philosophy generator doesn't concern itself with coffee tables or computers because their paradigms are unilateral. We want to wonder about ourselves, as choosers.

Experiential Norms, that is, paradigm that are set by your experiences, are what I refer to as being X in the Philosophy Generator. These are the norms of existence. They are both the naturally occurring and observed lessons of life that you can know, left to your own devices. X is the essence of existentialism. Of all the possible thoughts and experiences, free of influence, everyone can only have their own. They may or may not lay claim to their experiential norms, depending on their awareness of them, but they still have no choice but to have them, short of some vegetative state.

They cannot also have someone else's

experiences, (these must be shared.) One can have experiences similar to someone else, as for most of us love is, wholly or in part, similarly reciprocated. One can see the same movie as one's date and while still having quite similar experiences, it certainly cannot be called the same experience, in the strictest sense.

Experiential norm is to experience as social norm is to influence. Experiential norms are the associations made up independent of influence of someone else's paradigms. Social norms are, in the most general terms, the opposite: Paradigms that you have made directly from the influence of others. These are the products of interactions with others. You may or may not be having an experience to build such a social paradigm, the condition being met for it being S and not X is that you couldn't have had this experience alone. For instance: love is an experience that you sense, have, feel and definitely can properly define as being a paradigm built from X, yet, it simply cannot be without S. You require someone *to* love. The same could be said for the love of nation or pumpkin pie. It turns out it doesn't matter: unless you are a nation of one or invented pie these are examples of social norms. Love is an abstract paradigm that can be made up of many associations from both sides of the philosophy generator. An example of a more concrete variety, such as "fire hurts" while possibly built from experience, (burning one's self,) could also be Social (having been instructed.) We are not yet ready to define what "love" is, nor do we need to in order to make our point: Whether the paradigm being considered is seemingly as complicated as "love" or as apparently simple as "fire burns" it can and often will be built from both S and X.

It could be that you've learned of fire from benign associations such as those previously mentioned or you could have watched your parents burn to death when you were four, sometimes it's not what we learn but how we learn it that speaks to the power of the paradigm. There are also, as in the case of the child who watches his parents die in a fire, possibilities for influence to build paradigm, despite the intention of the parents themselves. Whether or not influence is intentional and regardless of it being subliminal we only care to be aware of it, controlling any power it might have over us. It is to be expected that certain extreme paradigms are more influential than others, there is no reason to suffer from indefinite interference unless you lead the unexamined life. We must continue to ponder the two essentials: Influence and experience.

Our next term in the generator is L, for learned. To learn something is to absorb, develop and remember a paradigm. It is the processing of new data. There are many different ways to learn things and two very different L's in our generator. In the simplest sense, you can either learn something, with or without the influence of others. Every Social norm, every S paradigm is a Learned paradigm. So where you may have learned from first hand experience that fire is hot and what a burn is, it is unlikely that you would develop the idea that an offering to the God(s) should be a burnt sacrifice, without having some sort of Social influence. (Yet, at some point, obviously, someone must have ultimate authorship of the idea.) An area where the definition of a social norm is such as this, becomes easy to recognize as being social. If, for instance, you were taught by someone else that iron could be heated to the point where as, when pressed against an open wound, cauterization could occur, this too would seem to be an SL paradigm. It can be, but there are multiple levels of associations possible for this "Cauterization" paradigm: You could have just "heard about it," and had no direct experience with it, IE: you never saw it work, never had it happen to you. You could have required it to save your life and very painfully experienced it directly. Either way, it is a Learned paradigm.

The difference is Social norms that *can* be experienced fall into the L that resides in the middle, connected to both S *and* X, experience and influence. Social norms that cannot be experienced *must* go into the L on the right side of the philosophy generator, dangling by themselves, products of only ideas. At some point in time, one individual came to understand the utility of cauterization, how is irrelevant, but for him, that was a learned experiential paradigm. When he shared that information with someone else and so from then on to unknown numbers of others, it became an SL.

Compare the discovery of cauterization with the realization that someone at some time developed the idea that burning a living creature alive might, in some way, influence unknowable yet feared forces for the better. It could very well be that the initiator of this "Sacrifice" paradigm did experience the idea as some sort of epiphany. Perhaps it was even a religious experience in the convincing sensory format of booming voice, burning bush. This, for that person, would be no less of an eXperiential norm. That is not what we are contesting, but rather that *because* the experiencer cannot share the direct experience that it must be defined as a Social norm. One cannot, at least as far as we are yet aware, deliver said booming voice or burning bush for others to assign as XL in the same way one can demonstrate cauterization. Therefore, we must take the bearer's word on the matter which, by definition, is what makes it and keeps it SL and furthermore, un-experienceable. It is, at the least, possible for cauterization to be XL. It can be said that the direct link to the source is what determines whether or not a learned social norm can be experienced directly and thus be more easily authenticated and evaluated.

Before we move on to the next symbol "N" let's take just a moment to be clear on the difference between learned social norms and learned experiential norms. We will, as per the standards of a doing philosophy, plumb the depths of each of our definitions soon enough. Having no proper understanding of words such as "experience" or even what it means to "know" something, one might think that there *must* be learned paradigms that are picked up by groups of individuals, simultaneously. For example, if we imagine a tribe of island dwellers, cut off from any other peoples, viewing, for the first time in their tradition, a solar eclipse. *All* of the tribe is seeing it at once and for the group, the eclipse is an learned social paradigm that they cannot recreate, *but* they each, individually had the experience as an XL. Contrast this with asking Bob if he loves Sally and vice versa. A recounting of love is as abstract as *tale* of a solar eclipse, yet because we are able to go to the source we can experientially learn the reality of what love means to the lovers. We cannot ask the moon what it means by passing in front of our sunlight, nor can we make it do so. If we live in a time or place where no one can rightly explain what an eclipse is, we have no hope of understanding the reality of the phenomenon.

Even if we *can* fathom the scientific nature of an eclipse, in our times and positions, we still must define our understanding of it as a Social norm, unless we have experienced one ourselves. Now imagine that you are that primitive island dweller and you are being told by your elders that you must sacrifice a virgin to the volcano so that it doesn't swallow the sun again. The relevance is revealed in the trust you have for the source and when you have experiential doubts as to someone else's social norm, evaluation is all you have. One can only know something through experience, otherwise it is essentially a belief. This distinction, as it will turn out, creates the opportunity for Anti-Social Engineering. All belief must be evaluated.

What is it we mean when we say an association, idea or piece of an idea is natural? By the requirement of the Philosophy Generator it must be, at least, be exclusive of something learned. We already know, or are expected to know that which is natural. We are all creatures of instinct. There are certain things that we are "hardwired" to know, to accept, to use. While it can properly be argued that there are natural paradigms that can be learned, it must not be that this is the case for the

Brian C. Taylor

philosophy generator, as it already has a category for learning, both with and without influence. It could be that you consider learning baseball as natural as learning to love, it isn't. Nature provides what we need inherently, the needs we create are unique, special and extraneous. As these provisions are separated in life, so are they in the Generator.

So let's now examine the far left of the Philosophy Generator's footing, where Paradigm is proven eXperiential and finally determined to be Naturally occurring. (Synonyms for which we can accept autoNomic or Necessary.) This category, by its associative ties, cannot have any social aspect to it. The types of paradigms that fall into this category are the things that without, we would not be possible, or if you prefer, the "Intrinsic Essentials" of a species. For eg: 1.) Pain hurts. (Pain has a purpose, it is a warning system to protect from harm.) 2.) Many species offspring are loved. (So they are cared for and protected. 3.) Lion's roars are intimidating. (So you avoid them.) 4.) You must hold your breath under water. On and on the list goes...

It does seem somewhat of a misrepresentation to suggest that all natural systems, or even species have any particular necessity that remains inherent in all members. So I'll remind you that we are particularly interested in the human psyche and the social interactions that stem from it as I gently prove to you otherwise, none the less. For, despite there being life forms on this planet that surely couldn't care less about one or more of the four above proposed necessities, I submit that, for all those beings and more, there will always be a set of rules that

21

existence will either insist upon or will come to accept. (For instance, a fish isn't going to care too much about holding his breath underwater but it has its own set of problems when the net pulls it up.) Thus when sourcing paradigm to be a naturally occurring experiential norm, one can confidently claim that to class as such, the association must be, if not necessary, then universally adopted or exemplary.

So that while the bio-mechanics of life tell us that "fire hurts," it is also no less instinctual or reasonable for us to behave exemplary, such as we care for our young and generally don't eat our spouses. Naturally occurring experiential norms develop necessary paradigms, because we have determined this in our definitions we may now all but completely disregard them, for what reason could we find to make evaluating them valuable?

It should be coming clear that we only really need to take a good look at our learned paradigms. Before we can continue it is of the utmost importance that we can appreciate the value in knowing the difference between the two types of learning illustrated by the philosophy generator. We must understand that no one can be teaching us these paradigms for them to be experientially learned. (For if someone was teaching us, while this would be an experience we were having, it must be considered in the S column, as it is not self-sourced, it is influence.) This might seem clear now but it is easy to forget later that these learned experiential norms are not the same things as learned social norms. Keep in mind the root letters of these concepts and what those letters symbolize. A learned experience is done on your own without Social interaction. Learned experiential norms are the lessons that experience has taught us, the things we've come to understand, alone. Remember, just because it's learned doesn't mean it's taught and just because you believe it doesn't mean you know it to be true.

Learned experiential paradigms are secondary to our Naturally occurring norms because all humans have N, they are necessary! The development of experiential paradigms, by the limitation of not being N means that each individual person is going to have unique results. So while N tells you pain hurts, L tells you that fire is hot. Where X and N say offspring are loved L teaches that you can love a spouse, a nation, a God. Where experience and nature say Lion roars are scary, a learned understanding can explain that where there are lions, there is meat. Finally, having to hold your breath underwater could lead to learning that said lion won't chase you into said water. We will shortly come to find that all paradigm can be connected in some way, with only the limitation of a Social norm that can't be experienced.

The philosophy generators' ability to classify paradigm and source provides a valid method to help evaluate the worth of a particular opinion, moral or position. Even from within our strict definitions and encompassing scope, the device is not an "answer machine." The mechanics of the PG will not always provide you with definitives. So, in our philosophy as in our lives, we must exercise our Assignee's Prerogative (the ability to assign meaning or value to any particular grouping of associations.) Once we begin examining the rules our definitions create the generators' utility becomes expanded somewhat.

I must point out that we are, at this time, dismissing defining the final term in the generator: U, save to say that it, through a complexity requiring its own definition, for now will be put as "that which is good, right or true" and specifically not the opposite. If you prefer you may think of U, for now, as being generally positive and ~U as being generally negative. U stands for eudaemonia which is a Greek word and idea, first commented upon by Aristotle in the *Nicomachean Ethics* and we will address it in depth soon enough.

Brian C. Taylor

4
the Psychology of
the Philosophy Generator

The reason we are even capable of asking "of what are my thoughts made?" is through our understanding and facility of Superego, Ego and Id. It would be impossible if we weren't beasts able to "step outside" to examine ourselves. (Incidentally, I believe that this fact alone makes our existence deserving. We have,by way of this ability, the chance to achieve the opportunity for perfection.)

Ego is the mediation between the conscious and the subconscious. It is your perception of reality, both what you experience and think about and what is beyond your understanding, but no less influential. Your ego knows your consciousness and feels your subconsciousness. That means that basically you are your ego, built out of your paradigms. Your Id is your innate primary instincts. Thoughts of fight or flight come from the id, beyond your subconscious, past what you've leaned in this life, to what all humans (all creatures) are pre-wired to know. (I know there is an argument for plant life having id, and even ego, but there is also an argument for animals having superego and we don't have the time, nor the need, to cover everything.) It should be noted that humans add to our id as we go, it is not purely a device of instinct. Paradigms, as we build them, store them and think about them, become part of our consciousness. The memory, (thought) becomes a part of our operations and then is forgotten, an imperceptible piece of the filter through which we view all future paradigm, a place to react from. All additions to the id, however, are products of our experiences and as such, may or may not be eudaemonic. We of course presume that the exemplars we accept are worthy and that they steer us correctly, but how many of us ever consider the presence of the phenomenon?

Superego is the term used to indicate the conscious determination of ego. It is the little voice in our head that asks us "What do we think we're doing?" when we're doing something wrong. Where ego knows our consciousness and only feels our subconscious, the superego knows both. Where the ego can be faulted by a misinterpreted bias hidden in a memory, superego knows that bias already and can compensate for it. By understanding and exploring superego we discover all our secrets, all our "why's." Assignee's Prerogative is a method to appreciating your superego, your "rule construct." (It has been said that your superego is like your parents, tagging along inside your brain.) When we say, "I am ashamed of myself," the superego is ashamed of the ego. By deciding the worth of paradigms based on full disclosure of what those paradigm are and why they came to be, we have created the possibility for a Superego type Awareness. The next achievement to strive for after mastering your superego is superconsciousness, the recombination of the conscious and subconscious minds. (Or perhaps with a Universal form.) But I'm digressing to the point of sounding like one of the purveyors of Authentic Self from the non-empirical camp. Let's agree that it is possible for our determinism to stem from a place of thorough contemplation and that our biology is responsible for us being able to do so.

Id, in the generator falls into the category of experiential norms, or, as "id paradigms" are experienced and expected, they are natural experiential norms. They are unavoidable and therefore, we cannot change them ourselves. They have to be changed biologically within the totality of the species. This is beyond our control and examination of these automations, while perhaps fruitful in creating an understanding of self, will never lead to associations your ego has formed. The examination of naturally occurring experiential norms is pointless, they are always necessary. (With the possible exception of social engineering or some other unknown reprogramming of the id.) Ego and superego, obviously run the gamut the generator has to offer, can equally steer us right or wrong and can be experienced by yourself or shared through the influence of others. Having an understanding of paradigm, knowing the importance of contemplating source and hopefully, beginning to have an appreciation for philosophy, let's take this opportunity to dive into the philosophy generator. It is through this simple device that our argument becomes evident and by discovering the products of our definitions we are enlightened to its utility.

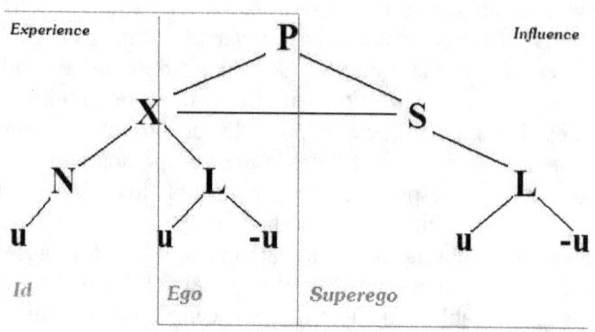

Brian C. Taylor

5
the Logic of the
Philosophy Generator

There are some things about these topics defined by the Philosophy Generator that can be said for certain, we will call these things rules. In the Philosophy Generator we have letters to symbolize ideas and lines to associate those ideas with others. Our concern with these lines, that is to say, the *reason* for which we examine these associations, is to extract their origin.

So it can then be said that, for the PG, if we are in agreement that a.) The terms defined are all inclusive and mutually exclusive. (For instance: It is true that there is no S that is N, nor N that is ~U or there is no P that isn't either X or S unless it is also L) and b.) The definitions and associative links are accurate and relevant (IE. If we are correct, complete and theoretically sound); then we have every right to draw conclusions from the rules created by the Philosophy Generator. So let's do that.

1.) Paradigms, are groups of associations built from either experiential or social norms or some combination thereof.
P > (X v S) v (X . S)

If it's P then it's (X or S) or (X and S.)

Our ideas about everything are determined either by us or for us. This, in and of itself, is quite enough of a pill for some people to swallow. What I would consider a very obvious fact can be nothing short of unbelievable to others. This is the foundation upon which every other conclusion we'll make is built.

Other philosophers, some friends of mine, would contest this starting point and if they were able to either prove or disprove the existence of "free will," might think they could crush my argument and win the day. The question of free will asks, "Are we able to exercise control over our decisions or is everything determined?" The Philosophy Generator says the answer is "Both."

You do have the ability to direct your choices, both consciously and unconsciously and you have determined traits that must be followed. There is a boundary set here determined by the rules of existence. As such, the options within the boundary are finite but those options are numerous, indeed *seemingly* infinite. The idea of will, is definitely in play and part of the Generator, the idea of freedom is not relevant to the discussion.

Ultimately, it is *because* Determinism insists that "events" (and therefore "ideas,") are caused by the needs of their predecessors that brings "freedom" into the equation. This is a causation that you can follow back as far as you care to. It is another one of those things that a person could devote an entire career exploring, many have. To put it simply, answer: "What situation could possibly arise where you wouldn't choose what you

Brian C. Taylor

must?"

Free will, in my opinion, is a mere question of responsibility, either you have it and take it, or you don't, the necessity of it is a matter of opinion. Despite our inability to know if we are the originators of our own thoughts or in control of our own beings or destinies we can understand the differences between paradigms built from either experiential or social norms. We can understand that we succumb to our will through our behaviours and that our motivations can be hidden from us. Our reality must be that we can only know what it is possible to while taking comfort in the exponential growth of what being possible encompasses.

2.) There is no such thing as a paradigm that is a naturally occurring social norm.

$S > \sim N$

If it's S then it's not N.

Social norms must be developed into a paradigm that is then shared. In contrast, an experience can just "happen," without the development of any paradigm, except the one being built by the experience itself and any new immediate associations. To argue that a grouping of individual experiences collect into a social experience is to defy our definitions. A group of individuals is not an individual any more than a grouping of individual experiences is one social experience.

A social norm is also built entirely from influence, an experiential norm is exactly the opposite, it cannot be both. To say the words "there is no such thing as a naturally occurring social norm," may seem obvious, even trivial by our definitions, until one considers the truth of what this means.

    3.) All social norms are engineered. Social norms that can't be experienced are not natural.

$S > L$

If it's S then it's L.

$(L .\sim X) > \sim N$

If it's L and not X then it's not N.

    A learned social norm is gained through instruction or influence. Instruction and influence are methods to design an outcome and that *is* engineering. It may or may not be a conscious effort to learn it on your part, or to teach it on their part, this is not at issue as one can be aware of being instructed without knowing of motives as easily as one can pass on lessons learned without understanding the possible implications of the lessons and vice versa.

    Intention does have its place in our considerations and will be given its due diligence soon enough. It is not our place to speak to the motives of the engineers, nor may it even be possible. For what if we have engineered a particular paradigm ourselves? It is certainly possible for an individual to concoct any number of incorrect ideas. (How many times in your life have you improperly deduced what someone seemed to be implying?) It might seem that this "Accidental Engineering" seems ill-defined, perhaps impossible, but we are not speaking of blueprints or locomotives, only paradigms. Our thoughts and ideas are "built" from something: What we have learned we have contrived, this is what we have built in our minds, either by ourselves or with others, either intentionally or not, either with

Brian C. Taylor

awareness of it, or not.

Ultimately we will find that the judgement of the source's intention or associative effectiveness is up to you. The only thing to be concluded by accepting this rule as a reality is that everything we have learned outside our experiences has, at the least, the same likelihood of being necessary as not and, if we are able to point to engineering, it is probably because we have discovered some result to have been engineered.

Every paradigm we can build from experiential norms has the potential to be influence free as a natural necessity. We can have "engineered experiences," by learning things either through observation, (influence,) or through lesson, (instruction,) but we can also learn things on our own. Once someone else's paradigms are involved, it must be a social norm and the potential for necessity is diminished. If experiencing the social norm is impossible, if it is a lesson that you can neither test nor prove, the opportunity for potential necessity becomes zero. This is not to call into question the worth of any particular social norm, it simply means that one loses the opportunity to prove the paradigm natural by its lack of any experiential quality.

In a very real way the influence of social norms is the most predominant threat to your happiness, authenticity, productivity and promotion. Regardless of the motives of the influencer it is your awareness or lack of it that will determine your ability to adjust, absorb, deny or combat any particular paradigm. If you aren't aware of any particular paradigm's influence on your own ideas, if you cannot even realize its existence and/or power, you are unable to do anything other than succumb to it. Sometimes this inability will pose no threat to you or your ideas about things, such as in the case of someone teaching you how to play a particular game. Contrast this idea with the more detrimental and powerful realization that someone has been playing games *with you*. Whether it's a friend, employer, teacher, advertiser or government, influence is everywhere, without contemplation and evaluation you have no way of knowing if said influence is worthy of adoption.

Let us not fail to notice the relevance of the implications made by the fact social norms cannot be considered N. This is not a comment on the "naturalness" of societies to adopt particular behaviours based on biology, habit or necessity. (For instance, it's highly unlikely that, considering our current evolutionary model of existence, homosexuality could move to becoming the preference of the human species. However, it is quite easy to imagine a biological scenario where this outcome would be more likely.) When we say that a social norm cannot be naturally occurring we mean that the universality of necessity is an individual's experience. Any determined social necessity would be a matter of opinion, or it would already exist.

4.) Nature provides what is necessary, which is good.

N > U

If it's N then it's U.

We needn't get into a definition of eudaemonia beyond that of our previously stated generalizations of "good" and "bad" to express the importance of this rule.

Brian C. Taylor

It should be stated that we are, in this rule, like in all possible comments on the Philosophy Generator, speaking only of paradigm. To argue that all possible natural phenomena are "natural" or that all natural phenomena are "good" is not our concern. We are not seeking to debate any "Naturalistic Fallacy," nor at this point, even what "good" is. For the most part, it is for you to decide what is eudaemonic.

When we speak of N, we are only saying that there are paradigms that fit into our definition of what N is. Other, learned paradigms we can, or at least could, have an opportunity to change. With N, we have no choice. Like many philosophical concerns we are more impressed by what the statement doesn't say. As stated previously, naturally occurring experiential norms are required by us. There is no need to evaluate *that which existence insists upon*. (Which, incidentally, is a great definition for "nature.")

We need only evaluate that which we can dismiss as not being N, such as L. N is safe. Therefore, as N is necessary and automatically eudaemonic, it seems that it is only the things we learn that can pose any threat to our potential for U, for goodness, for rightness.

The reason we are unable to simply state that all possible experiences are not automatically eudaemonic is that we are just as able to trick ourselves as we are to be programmed by others. One would think that we would be less likely to fall prey to our own illusions and delusions than to those of someone else.

Let us compare two naturally occurring experiential norms that share a human commonality and

the Authentic Self

convenient illustrative properties: Fear and love. Surely we can all agree that these paradigms, whatever they might be for each individual, are extremely universal and naturally occurring phenomenon and this is true not only of humans. However, when we consider the irrational or damaging behaviour we exhibit in the name of fear and love, how can we doubt emotive potential to expose our weaknesses? Consider the man who wants to punch his ex-girlfriend's new beau in the face and the patriot who joins the army, are they not moved by their emotives? Do these paradigms not present real and common dangers?

6
Assignee's Prerogative & Hyper-Manipulation

If every Social Norm is engineered and it is what we learn that present the biggest dangers to our eudaimonea, then it is only the social aspects of the Philosophy Generator that provide the greatest utility and hope for our understanding of the self. If every socially engineered paradigm is an intention, we will be best served to reduce that intention to a command, such as: sacrifice the virgin to appease the sun god, support the troops, or buy Coca Cola because it makes for good times.

It goes without saying that we, short of becoming an expert on everything, must take the word of others in many, many cases. This brand of social engineering, a sort of universal or general movement that courses through a society, is as old as society. This is found in things like jurisprudence or morality. Accepted, instilled ideas such as that "murder had best be judged upon," or that "faith must be directed to a particular set of options" are rules of old. It is certainly not the case that these considerations are less powerful or dangerous than what we fear from modern methods of social engineering.

the Authentic Self

It is just that these methods are blatant. They insist upon themselves, "You will do this. You will act thus." etc. Some types of social engineering, regardless of source, simply tell you what it wants you to do or not to, think or not think. "Law A exists to control result B." These kinds of obvious controls are widespread throughout society, down to your family organization. They are, for the most part, a necessary component of any healthy social organization. We shall call this type **Transparent Social Engineering** because we are told what the "rules" are and *they are what they are.* (They are not a secret, nor a lie, nor a trick.)

This does not mean that there aren't hidden motivations for what appears to be transparent social engineering, regardless of its age, type or dispersal methods. The example of human caused climate change, although somewhat controversial, is only controversial because of the distance between the empirical science of it and the layman. Consider the Catholic prohibition of birth control and the "suggestion" that people go forward, be fruitful and multiply. The prohibition is subject to punishment, the suggestion is not, although it is suggested that being "fruitful" would be rewarded. The suggestion, taken in context, could easily be determined to present the idea that there is both a need and ability presented by our existence, to multiply. The prohibition, disguised as the will of God and implicating both "his" desires and eliminating the option by creating a rule, carries with it an intention. Some may argue that this intention is simply in keeping with nature, but intention is only half of social engineering, the other half is made up of results. For if there are no results, the engineering will just change to what produces results. (These engineers don't give up easily.) The result of contraception being banned for Catholics is, of course, a whole lot more Catholics. I am not commenting on the "rightness" or "wrongness" of this intention, nor am I even saying that this *product is the intention of the rule.* This is just the result of the engineering and no one can deny that. I also feel it safe to assume that the results, if placed in obvious intentional statements, put the proof in the pudding, so to speak. However, nowhere in the Bible does it say, "We need to have a bunch of Christian babies so that we can outnumber those "other" babies. This is **Semi-Transparent Social Engineering.** We are clear on the engineering, not on the "why." We must make a decision, based on a decision. We are somewhere in between assignee's prerogative and hyper-manipulation. (Hyper-manipulation is simply pre-programming to accept later paradigm.)

Think back to when you were a little child, leaning the lessons we all do. Perhaps you had a parent or teacher who didn't bother to always explain the "why" to you. They might just say, "Because I said so." (An appeal to authority.) This is a short term solution. It's short not because the statement is brief, but because you are present. The child can easily ask, "What do you mean? Why can't I have another cookie?" (Or, if he or she is really clever, "Why do you say so?") What does "I say so" mean? It must mean, "my saying so is enough to answer your 'why,' because there really is no answer, or I don't want you to know it." However, what if your parent lied and said, "The cookies are all gone." Here we would have a case where the parent said something, rather than nothing, yet it is just as valueless to you as "because I said so." You still have no cookie. The only difference is now we're not bugging Mom for another cookie, we believe her when she says there are no more and we understand what "no more" means. This is a small example of **Opaque Social Engineering.** (Opaque is the opposite of transparent.) Here we enter the domain of the strict social norm, the place where we don't know what we're basing our paradigm building on. It could be a lie, it could be nothing, unknown or arbitrary. Let's not forget, social engineering is goal oriented.

    The "transparency" of social engineering is how I describe the difference between persuasion and manipulation. When one is persuaded, by a social norm one has been given an intention and can make a choice. However, if one is misinformed, makes a choice based on that information, thereby making an inauthentic decision, or is unaware of the choice being made, then one has been manipulated. If what is being manipulated, (paradigm or association of,) is an idea that was inherent in the first place, hyper-manipulation has taken place. The engineer, in the case of hyper-manipulation, is working a programme of a programme.

    So, again, we find the importance of asking "why?" Just like when we consider the source of paradigm with the philosophy generator we can discover our "why's," so too can we by examining our social engineering. Our first clue to the engineers can be found by who's delivering the message. If it's a beer commercial, you're safe to assume that there is a semi-transparent manipulation taking place. The advertisers are not trying to *persuade* you that drinking their brand will make you seem sexy and interesting. For this they would require a plan of **Long Term Social Engineering.** This type of persuasive plan is Transparent, or at least Semi-Transparent, such as "Jay walking is illegal, or "Catholics should multiply." In contrast to this, **Short Term Social Engineering** must be more aggressive in their methods. The climate change argument is an example of an aggressive bit of social engineering. You can tell when an intention is being aggressively sought by how repetitious, present and explanatory it is. If you're going to be transparent about your persuading, you've got to deliver a lot of "why." This "lot of why" is a measurement of **Force.**

Now, if you're not going to be transparent, if you're not using **Persuasive Social Engineering** you don't have to explain a damn thing. If you're using **Manipulative Social Engineering** you need not present any "why" if you don't want to. Or you can lie, use misdirection, such as the things that lead to the second Gulf war. When the American officials stated that there were "weapons of mass destruction" in Iraq, they weren't being transparent. In social engineering, whenever you are not transparent, you are not persuading, you are, via

your secrets, or repetitious force, manipulating, (in the short term.) When the message is "Support the troops" it has been repeated so often and so ingrained since the end of the Vietnam war, (force) that it moves into hyper-manipulation by sheer repetition. Force trumps transparency when there is enough power and time behind it. So there seems to be a ratio that we can express between transparency and force, they are directly proportional. The less of one means the more of the other.

Manipulative Social Engineering is our main typification of concern as it is the most damaging. It is opaque and secret. As we are able to deliberate ourselves the intentions that we can experience, we are most interested in the "S" side of the Philosophy Generator. As we have already proven that all social norms are engineered, we shall now attach an association of (e) for Engineering to our S in the PG. Underneath that, as we have determined social engineering, S(e) to be either Persuasive or Manipulative, we will divide S(e) into P2 or M. (The P has a 2 after it because we already have a P term in "Paradigm.")

We know that at least one of the determinants differentiating persuasion from manipulation is a measurement of force versus transparency, so let's put that in too, the first box, "t\f." In fact, now that we are ready to do some real Anti-Social Engineering, let's put everything in and go through the steps. We've already established an expectation for S(e) and we've noticed it in our lives in some fashion, let's assume we we're satisfactorily able to reduce and identify it as a socially engineered paradigm lacking an experiential quality. Since we can't experience it we must contemplate it some other way. If we could experience it, the intention would be connected to X and our determinations of eudaemonia would be simple.

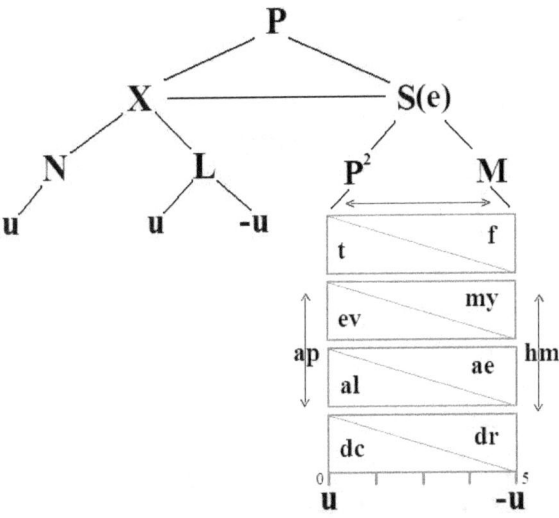

After the social engineering is split into either persuasion or manipulation it falls into the series of four sets of proportional measurements, (the boxes.) Taken together, the boxes are the eudaemonic scale. The first of them is the measurement of transparency vs force. We say versus because they are directly proportional. The transparency works from its high side, on the left, to its low side on the right. The force works in the opposite direction. (Ignore the little 0 and 5 on either side at the bottom, look to the size of the triangle that contains the letter t. It is larger on the left. For f it is larger on the right.) The less t, the more f and vice versa. This explains the right/left movement of the chart.

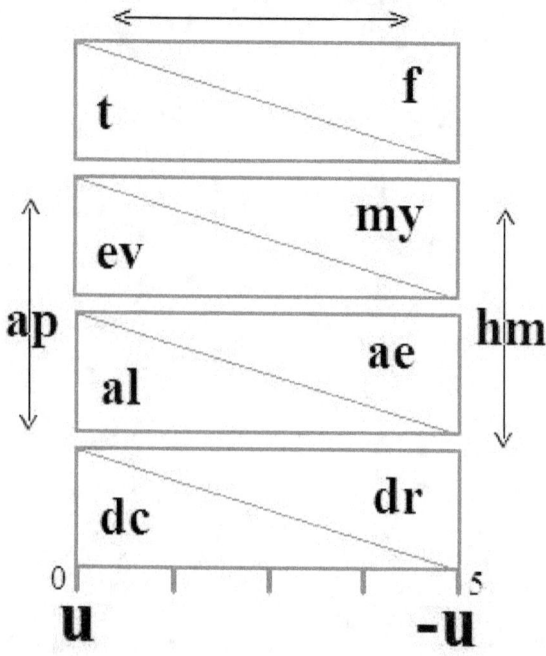

On the left side, we see an up/down arrow. As we move through these connected boxes, working toward the bottom, any results that fall left of centre are said to be ap, which we remember as assignee's prerogative. ("I have the ability to assign whatever importance to my paradigms.") Thus, if we wish to have a high degree of ap, the first box tells us transparency trumps force. We might be somewhere in the middle in our determinations and call it "semi-transparent" or have an extreme lack of transparency and call it "opaque." (Remember "it" is the intention, the S(e) be it Persuasion or Manipulation, or some combination of both, from your point of view.) It is the directionality of paradigm, which ultimately will end at P, at the top, a grouping of associations.

On the right side, we see a corresponding up/down arrow with the letters hm, which you may have guessed is for hyper-manipulation. (Programming to prepare for future deciding.) To be hm is to not be ap and vice versa. At the bottom is our old friend u, for eudaemonic or eudaemonia, which we will continue to "dumb down" to "good, right or true." So then, having assignee's prerogative is preferable to being hyper-manipulated. It is a fundamental question of freedom. On this point, we must agree.By "transparency", we mean "the amount that we are aware of the true intention" of the social engineering. (Is the command or intention actually saying what the desired result is?) There are two considerations when attempting to evaluate the t of any intention: Is there an Intention in Action and does it match the Prior Intention? (Are they saying "something" and does what they say match up with what they are "really asking for?") A stop sign is a stop sign, a Coke may or may not teach the world to sing, there is no possible way that the Army can help you be all that you can be, unless it kills you.

By "force" we mean "the amount of insistence

and repetition." Such that a stop sign is extremely repetitious, widespread and exemplary, as well as being insistent to the tune of a hundred dollar fine and possible accident. One idea that is much less apparent is the quiet force of constant repetition. Force can require time to take effect as we may be eased into an idea, perhaps over the course of several decades. Force asks, "How adamant is the (e)?

Our next box is the ev\my which contain the terms, "Evaluability" and "Mystery" Evaluability is a term I have stolen from economics. For our purposes it is *your awareness of the actual intention* and *your ability to think well about it.* This may sound a little similar to transparency but ev is reliant on the measurement before it. Without knowing something of the transparency and force one would have nothing to evaluate. Each of the boxes is a subset of the one above it. This order is intentional. Evaluability isn't us asking how transparent the social engineer is being, it is us asking ourselves, "with the amount of t\f I've got and with *who I am,* how well am I able to evaluate the intention?" We are aware, we may or may not be correctly aware. How correctly aware are we? What do we know about this intention in the first place? Do we have experience? Are we an expert? Do we have no idea what we're thinking about? These are the things that raise our level of evaluability.

Evaluability reduces when it becomes taken for

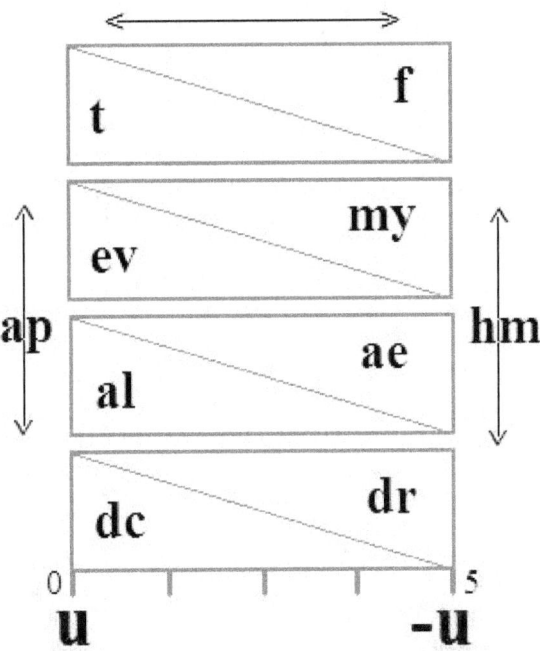

granted, moved into the background. So, in the long term, we might stop evaluating a particular paradigm as it becomes exemplary. Or we might have just decided that we think this way or that way because "everyone else does," without evaluating the virtue of our choice. (This would most likely still need time.) When ev reduces, the user (that's you, the person using the Philosophy

Generator,) becomes less able to think about and less able to understand the intention. This, of course, can lead to the intention being less thought about and less understood, thus increasing mystery. This is fine for things like soft drinks but when we answer important questions without thinking, at all, ever, we have a problem. Mystery represents the unknown. When we don't know about what it is we are dealing with, when we aren't aware there is *anything* to deal with, we are dealing with a mystery.

At this point in the PG we have evaluated, to the best of our ability, how much we can honestly determine about the intention. The next step is to ask "How do I feel about it?" I'm not presuming that feeling is not thinking, but rather there is but one inexorable fact in the distinction: there can be thinking without feeling but there can be no feeling without thinking. We are not capable of *anything* if not for our ability to think. The necessity of feeling seems to be a natural byproduct of the social community. We would be remiss to not include the feelings we have, particularly in the middle of this exercise. This is what makes the Philosophy Generator what it is: It is you, telling yourself who you are. You give it the only power it has. (So be honest.) We have earned the right to feel the feelings we do through our being able to achieve this level of mental functioning. Don't forget, you and I, are not flying off the cuff right now, we are not on the battlefield or yelling at our televisions, we are *dismantling thought.* Anyone bothering to go to this much trouble making a decision on any particular paradigm deserves to claim that he or she truly did their best. Being well feels good.

The next box is measuring the appeal to logic versus the appeal to emotion. This box asks us to consider the degree to which the intention appeals to either what we react to or what we agree to. Emotions, as we have stated, are to be expected and respected, but we must think of them as something that happens *to us*. They well up inside us and overtake us, at least sometimes. What we wish to notice from within our Philosophy Generator is

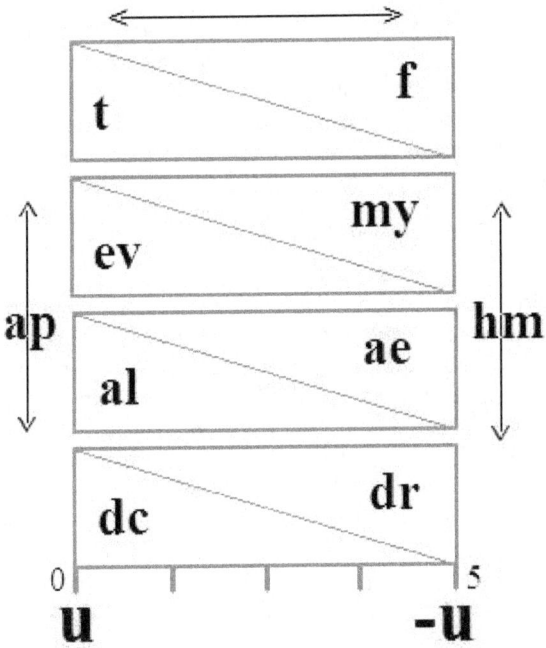

what we are reacting to. If you find yourself yelling angrily at a politician on the news, there's a reason. If you find yourself crying at a movie, there's a reason. You are probably not, however, crying because of a stop sign or angry because they have Pepsi instead of Coke. (I did say "probably.") In terms of the "measurement" of emotion, simply ask, "How strongly do you feel about the (e)?"

The logical side of the equation is a little more complicated as we must consider **Simplicity and Consistency.** To do this we must do some choosing that is directly related to whether or not we think the intention "makes sense." The more complex or variable we find the intention the more simplicity is reduced. Thus, even though you might not find a generalized intention, such as "Communism is wrong," to be particularly emotional to you, it is far too complex and has too many variables to appeal to your logic and must score heavily on the ~u side. A stop sign is going to score very high on the appeal to logic side of the scale, its message is in no way convoluted or random. The Coke commercial would not score as eudaemonic in the al/ae box, unless it featured a finely dressed middle aged man, looking like someone you could trust and he said, "Listen, you all know what Coke is. We'd like you to continue buying it. Next time you feel like having a delicious carbonated beverage, why don't you make it a Coke?" Instead the commercial says "Coke is" this or that. The Coke man couldn't come out and deliver a logical message because there are hundreds of colas out there, it simply wouldn't work. This is why attachments to fun, love, sex, the things we enjoy, are the associations engineers wish to use. This is why some intentions are entirely appeals to emotion.

Notice that the al\ae box is not asking "is the intention logical" nor "is it emotional?" It is, once again, asking *you* "does this intention *appeal* to your logic? How much? And your emotion? How much?" There is a consideration of the message itself, such as we know a Coke commercial *must* attach itself to emotion to be effective, as does the army recruitment ad. However

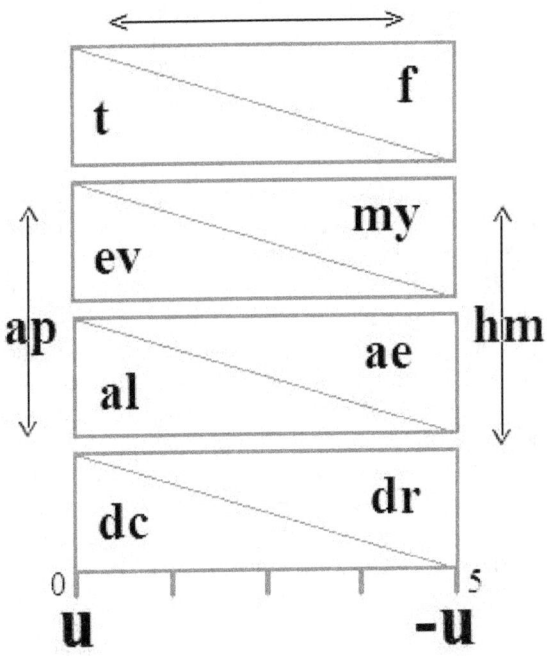

appeals to logic are no less commonplace. There are countless examples of arguments made: perhaps the Mayor of your town thinks you need a new bridge, he's going to make the case for its construction as reasonable as possible. He might try to throw a little emotion in there, say something like, "It will make it easier for commuters to get home to spend more time with their families." (Especially if "families first" was the phrase of the day.) For the most part, the Mayor's argument is going to be based on facts and figures, however doubt-able they may or may not be. When you are part of a team, say the crew of a naval ship, you are not following orders on the basis of your passions, you follow them because you understand the logic in keeping them followed.

Logic, unlike emotion, is not something that happens *to us*. Logic does not "well up inside and take over us." Therefore logic must explain things and reason with us. Where emotion is used to make something more than what it is, logic is used in an attempt to reveal what it is. The problem here, which we have evaluated in the boxes above to the best of our abilities, is the accurate interpretation of the *actual* intention. Such is it that we consider one politician's lies atrocious and another politician's lies desirable. At this point in the PG we are beginning to point to latent desires within us. By finding a particular argument logical, we express a lesser version of the same intentionality that emotions evoke.

Our final box is our final say. The dc\dr box is simply a conclusion we must come to after all our deliberations. It is the "desire to concur" versus the "desire to resist." Consider this box a judgement free

Brian C. Taylor

zone. Although it is true we have come to some conclusions along the way, in the end, everything is up to the individual anyway, so tell the PG what *you* want, despite any emotion or logic. What do you desire to do with the particular socially engineered paradigm we are considering? You can have any reasons for the desire, we don't even care to know what they are. They needn't even correspond with any of the above boxes. If you desire to believe that the moon is made of green cheese, you go right ahead! You're entitled to believe whatever nonsense you like. The only stipulation I have for this final box, is that you remember you are desiring to concur with or resist the intention *as you originally reduced it.* We must not, for instance, be asking ourselves if we agree with the intention of "support the troops but not the war" if we have previously determined this to be impossible. Don't forget, the intention is in the form of a command: "Do this," or "think this." So the desire to concur or resist is not about the idea of the intention, but speaks to what the intention asks of us.

Now, if we ask ourselves, at this point, "Why do I desire to concur or resist any particular paradigm?" we are likely to find only a circular answer. "It is my desire to desire so." As I stated in the "rules" this is allowed. However, I think we can do better by understanding an as of yet un-discussed aspect of eudaemonia, that which makes the intention promotive. This is not "promotion" which is obviously built into the fact that you are aware of the intention at all. The idea is promoted by the Engineers. An idea is promotive when it *works for you.* We will discuss this idea in detail next chapter, for now, understand that we desire to concur with any particular intention when we are able to appreciate "what is in it for us."

Finally, at the very bottom of our now complete Philosophy Generator, we have u at the 0 side and ~u at the 5 side. Now, I never actually intended for there to be any method of quantifying the amount of u in any paradigm. When I first began thinking about this it was purely to be a methodology for the sake of method. What I originally was seeking was an understanding of *how* I was who I was. Perhaps how we all, become what we are. What made up, especially, the things that I found myself believing for no apparent reason. What was that reason? What if I am unable to determine if I'm right or wrong to think a certain way about certain ideas? I feel now that the PG is a solid path to answering these questions. The point is, I think it's silly to want to measure your own ideas about your programming, in any mathematical way. The habit of living contemplatively is it's own reward. However, it is possible to "score" your paradigms on an eudaemonic scale, which is what the PG boxes represent. I also expect that some of you will want to do so. This typification is something we seem to require, perhaps for distinction. At any rate, I won't belittle anyone for saying "My troop support paradigm gets a 6 on the eudaemonic scale." (Although, I probably wouldn't want to talk to you about war, unless I was seeking a debate.) One possible application of having such a distinction would be that, if used honestly, it could be a shortcut to understanding certain aspects of a person's morality. Simply make a note of where you scored each box on the scale from 0 to 5.

The lower the score, the better the thinking on any particular paradigm, therefore, the better your ability to choose rightly. (Assignee's prerogative.) The higher your score, the lesser your ability to think well on any paradigm, which interferes with your ability to choose rightly. (Hyper-manipulation.)

the Authentic Self

Brian C. Taylor

7
Eudaimonea

For something to be eudaemonic it must be conducive to our happiness. It is not *just* our "happiness" because there are connotations attached: success, fulfilment, flourishing, promotion, evolution, action and contentment. In ancient Greek, "eu" is "well" and "daemon" is "spirit." So it could be said we have room for interpretation. There is the philosophical movement of Eudaemonism, which is a system of ethics that puts a moral value on the likelihood of actions producing eudaemonia. Then there is eudaemonia itself, which is often incorrectly described as "happiness." I've described it throughout the book as roughly equivalent to "good, right or true." However, "happiness" alone does not completely define what eudaemonia is, nor even what it means to be happy. My generalization of "good, right or true," is also lacking. In this chapter we will attempt to redefine eudaemonia as the worthy goal of anti-social engineering, a pathway to virtue, as well as a quantification of the value of any particular paradigm. In order to do this we must develop an appreciation for the Aristotle's ethics and refine his philosophical habit of contemplation.

We have Aristotle to thank for our ideas about

eudaemonia and ethics in general. Although he names his treatise "the Nicomachean Ethics," after his Father Nicomachus, Aristotle was a student and contemporary of Plato, who in turn was a student of Socrates. (Much of Plato's work was actually the teaching of Socrates in dialogue form. Socrates never wrote anything down.) Aristotle was immeasurably influential to all the sciences due to his ability and desire to deconstruct and quantify. In fact, before Plato and Aristotle, *the scientific method itself didn't exist*. Aristotle, or Ari, as I will sometimes call him, is the Grandfather of defining, comparing and contrasting ideas. He is the inventor of the practise of doing philosophy and developed the foundation for which all logic is built.

When we discuss the Nicomachean Ethics, we are looking at Aristotle's ideas on what the purpose of life is and how to go about living it. In his estimation, which, with minor adjustments, we share, Ari believes that all of us seek "the good life." This good life is a product of our actions and everything seeks happiness. However, not everyone agrees on what makes them happy. Aristotle believes that the good life is sought by having a good spirit, which is something that can be developed with effort and time. Ethics are the study of bare principles and this is something we can practise. Virtue is the ability to choose "rightly" when considering alternatives, so too can we develop the habit. Aristotle delivers in his Ethics a practise that seeks what he calls the Golden Mean, a balance between excess and deficiency. He believes that like a horseman becomes excellent at his skill through practise, those seeking virtue can also hone their skills.

Brian C. Taylor

He says, "We do not act rightly because we have virtue or excellence, but we rather have those because we have acted rightly. We are what we repeatedly do. Excellence, then, is not an act but a habit."

Let's start with the idea of happiness, what is it? How do we find it? Aristotle asks us to examine things we choose for their own sake and things we choose for delayed rewards. (For him, being able to make this distinction explains a lot about what makes humans unique from other animals.) Ari argues that if you were to pursue everything you desired to its end, you will always wind up considering your happiness. For example, if someone asked me, "What would you do with ten million dollars?" and pursued the answers I gave with, "Why? Why? Why?" I would always end up saying, "because it makes me happy." Something like this: "What would you do with ten million dollars?" I would buy a house. "Why?" So I could be comfortable and raise a family. "Why?" So I could love, be loved, share my life with people and pass something of myself onto the future. "Why?" Because it would make me happy. So happiness is not a means to an end, it is the end. It is the desired result of whatever thought or activity taking place. Aristotle believes that all human activities aim to accomplish something we consider "good." Therefore, seeking something that is an end, in and of itself, such as happiness, should be an "ultimate good."

Being happy, for Aristotle is "good." Well, that's a start. He breaks the idea of "types of goods" into two groups: Apparent Goods and True Goods. **Apparent Goods** are the things we seek in life that may or may not lead to actual happiness. (The big boat, the expensive baubles, the promotion at work...) Don't confuse the idea of "good" with the idea of an object as a good. Good in this case is something we find eudaemonic, not merely existent. Apparent Goods can only provide pseudo-happiness. **True Goods** are real. So, as in the classic film, *Citizen Kane,* a grumpy old curmudgeon on his deathbed will come to realize that all of his wealth and power was for nought. He has missed out on the true goods of his life, in the pursuit of apparent goods. This means, of course, that we can be wrong about what we think is going to make us happy. This is particularly true when we become convinced by someone else of what will make us happy. (These we could call socially engineered goods.)

Still, "good" needs to become something standardized for us to all agree upon what it means. We all can determine our own pleasures, yes, but there must be some aspects of "goodness" that are definable. Aristotle says that everything has a function and the ability to perform that function well points to eudaemonia. You can, for instance, hammer a nail into a board with a flute but it is not going to work very well. Or, if you are a medical student, you might have a Professor who is an excellent Doctor but a horrible Teacher. Form, therefore, precedes function, but happiness is function living up to form. This is a key distinction that helps us separate eudaemonia from mere happiness. A flute cannot be "happy" or "unhappy" but its use as a hammer is definitely not eudaemonic. This harkens back to the Aristotelian definition of "essence." (A knife is not a knife if it has no edge, a chair is not a

Brian C. Taylor

chair if you can't sit in it, etc.)

So what is the human essence? We know our form quite well, what is our function? Ari, in his typical thoroughness, attempts to reduce this question to what humans are *able* to do, as what distinguishes us from other species. His answer is: Rationality, we are able to reason about what we know and choose. Specifically, because we are able to reason and other creatures are not, rationality *must* be our essence. Therefore, the good life is achieved by developing and exercising this ability.

Now, at this point, you might wonder about Ari's definition of rationality, or even reason, because many other animals can reason. This is true. A crow can solve multistage problems, build job specific tools and use them, all without being taught or otherwise having any previous experience with the particular skill set used. A crow, while a social animal, is certainly not on the same level as a man. This is true, so far. Herein lies the point, Aristotle, a huge fan of biology admittedly, was not an expert on everything. In fact, there are many aspects of *the Nicomachean Ethics*, as well as other works belonging to Aristotle, such as *the Politics,* that expose him to be, at least in part, a product of his times. (We shall not disparage him for this.) Ari's world is one where one knows his or her place. Women are lesser than men, but not quite "property." Slaves, be they male or female, are property, therefore cannot be citizens. This can be the only place where Aristotle's ideas can come from. He has no qualms about fashioning "the good life" for his time and place, specifically. It doesn't occur to him that the world may abolish slavery, or perhaps even that

61

exemplary ideas change. (Which is a rather odd thing to think about: If Aristotle can't remove the blinders we find limiting him a mere two thousand years later, can we remove ours in the present? Can we even identify our current blinders?) Humans are very fond of looking back and feeling superior. We need to reverse this process, to look forward *knowing* we're taking the right steps in the present, to get there. At any rate, we will take what we need from Aristotle and ignore his dustier ideas.

You might also have wondered about definitions of a word like "good." How are we going to define "good" when we can't even properly define "red" or "7"? The answer, which Aristotle reminds us of throughout his work, is "you can't." Everyone is different and what is good for the murderer may not be good for the milkmaid. Everyone must decipher their own ethics. Ari, in his "Doctrine of the Mean" is not unlike ourselves at this point, working through our own, private Philosophy Generator. The only thing that can be said about "goodness" is that it points to eudaemonia. Eudaemonia, in turn points to happiness, which seems to give us carte blanche. However, eudaemonia is not an end, such as mere happiness. Eudaemonia is an activity, a means to plural ends: Happiness and (something more.) We wish to define the "something more."

For the ancient Greeks, eudaemonism was apparent. If one walked through the streets of Athens in the time of Aristotle, the eudaemonic citizens would be vibrant, successful, friendly and energetic. This is why eudaemonia is not an inner, emotional state in such a way that mere happiness is, but to be eudaemonic is to put energy into action. One may find happiness in sitting around doing nothing all day, but it would be short lived. Even the laziest person in the world contemplates, (which is an action,) and has friends, relationships, etc. (At least, this is the case for healthy humans.) Thus, there is an active role for you to place in your eudaemonia, it is your choosing *and doing* well. Choosing well is the path to virtue. Doing well, acting rightly and being aware of it mark eudaemonia. If these definitions are true, then Aristotle is correct to deduce that they are *ongoing* exercises. It is a process, not a result. The result will always be varying degrees of virtue.

Previously, we used the following list of words in an attempt to describe and define the second aspect of "eudaemonia," beyond "happiness." Success, fulfilment, flourishing, promotion, evolution, action and contentment have been suggested, over the years, to fill the tangent that seems to represent "doing" more than "being," or the process more than the result. To this end, let us formally split our definition into two halves, the first being "happiness" which we define as "our pleasure to experience." (Let us, for the sake of clarity, further define "pleasure" as "the mental or biological response of positive feedback," and "experience" as "cognisance.") This "happiness" is subjective and relates directly to the experience itself. It is the "being" part of our definition. The second half of defining "eudaemonia," having to do with action and effort, carries an objective implication. It is this tangent that keeps eudaemonia from meaning "happiness" only. It is the "doing" part we must consider now.

the Authentic Self

Success, fulfilment and contentment are three forms of satisfaction. "Success", in modern parlance, is achievement. (It used to mean, "completion," be it good or bad.) Fulfil means "gain happiness or satisfaction," so we've found neither here. Contentment seems even weaker a definition. Let's throw all these weak words out. In fact, action and evolution are so non-directional that we don't even need to entertain them as candidates. What we need is something that speaks to our supposed purpose and lives up to our determined essence, namely our ability *to choose and act rightly.* The choice is not in question. We already know if we're satisfied! Our definition of eudaemonia needs to address what is happening that does the satisfying.

Flourishing is probably the most commonly attached appendage to "happiness" when defining what Aristotle meant by eudaemonia in the Nicomachean Ethics. I should point out, I'm not here attempting to interpret Ari's Ethics, nor what he means by any particular word he uses. I am attempting to end any and all question of interpretation. I define these terms for my purposes, which by now must be our purposes. (Best possible thinking.) Flourishing is a very good word, but it is less than perfect as the eudaemonic counterpart to happiness. To flourish is to grow or develop. This would seem to be "an ideal" that we could define as eudaemonic. It is certainly natural, even we ourselves have much experience with both growth and development. It seems admirable to pursue these things, in terms of gaining knowledge, which is something that Aristotle would agree. However, I think the scholars who have attached "flourishment" to eudaemonia have done so in error based on their understanding of Aristotle as someone who held contemplation in the highest regard. (Attaching -ment to a word indicates "the result of an action.") Flourishment, in the domain of our mental faculties, is obviously to be commended and, dare I say it, easily understood. We all can agree that having minds that grow and develop is desirable. Still, I must ask, so what? What about "flourishment" points to our objective onus to live up to the potential we have, as these creatures of reasonable essence? This is too specific an interpretation. It, once again, addresses the choice, not the choosing. Perhaps it was developed from the natural inclination for people to shy away from death. After all, it is disability, reduction, decay and finality awaiting us all, even just in terms of our mental faculties. By focusing on the results we are avoiding the action causing the results. I submit the suffix -ment is actually more important to this determination than any considerations of flourishing. Flourishing is as subjective a definition for eudaemonia as any of the previous words. We seem to be skirting the issue. Our essence is not to flourish, it is merely to reason. Even if we do it well we may or may not flourish.

Making up new words, such as "flourishment" is fair and sometimes necessary. "Flourishing as the result of an action," is tidy. Imperfect, but tidy. "Promotion" is a slightly better word because it simply means "activity that encourages." This again, seems to be pointing in the right direction without narrowing out "growth," or any other intention, as that which is being encouraged. Except here again, we must notice this "encouraging" also has an intention that may or may not prove eudaemonic. As usual, we must answer the basest possible question. What activity are we promoting? The simplest answer, the one that points to our essence, is the activity of rationalization. I submit we should be looking at the action itself. Being happy is something you can feel. Deciding that some particular action is going to make you happy takes contemplation. Eudaemonia can only be the product of being happy with your decision, even if the decision itself makes you unhappy. This can only be because you believe the decision you made was the right one. (The decision could still turn out to be a foolish one, what makes it "right" is contemplation. Doing your best. Trying.) If this is true, we could choose rightly and not flourish, or choose wrongly and flourish. Either case would still be eudaemonic because all we have to do is think about it in order to do our best choosing. A fool may come to flourish if fortunate but the pauper who has made the choices he has due to following his heart, (that which makes him happy) and his reason, (that which serves his purpose,) will be the one able to call his life, or any particular aspect of it, eudaemonic.

I would like to suggest that eudaemonia is *promotive*. **Promotive** is a word of my invention that means "acting on account of the reasons for doing so." The prefix "pro" comes from the Latin as a word that can mean "to replace." Such as, "in front of, in place of, on behalf of, on account of." "Motive" means "reason(s) for doing something." Thus, I have taken away the result orientated reason and replaced it with the act of the reasoning itself, achieving a much higher degree of

Brian C. Taylor

objectivity. It's not about the choice, it's about the choosing, as this is our forte. Contemplation is the only thing that can establish whatever choice you make. Reactions are not choices. Reactions may or may not make you happy, but they will never be eudaemonic. For something to be eudaemonic it will have to have been chosen. Thus, happiness can happen merely as a product of being human and eudaemonia must be achieved by finding virtue on the Golden Mean. Eudaemonia does not make you happy. Eudaemonia provides the happiness you feel *because* it's promotive. In a sense, one feels eudaemonic because one can recognize "the rightness of exercising one's essence." The effort is its own reward. Remember, it's pro*motive,* "acting on account of the reasons for doing so..." It's not a result, it's what leads to a result.

Now, you may have caught the apparent paradox present in my definition of promotive as a necessary constituent of eudaemonia. It is summed up well by the question, "Aren't all actions taken, done "on account of the reasons for doing so?" Yes, is the short answer, (although we could debate this question forever in the form of "free will vs determinism.) All actions are taken due to "whatever caused them" and there are certainly things "out there" in the world that we must deal with. Some of those things, as we well know, come in the form of an idea. When we deal with these ideas we, as humans, have *the ability to know we are dealing with them.* This is what solves the paradox: We may or may not know we are solving a certain problem, or making a certain choice, but *the option is there and it is this option that provides us our essence.* Eudaemonia is reserved for thought. It can only come to those who steer their intentions. Eudaemonia is yours to take, but you must take it. We do not ask the flute if it feels happy or purposeful being used as a hammer, because it is not a conscious being that can think. Eudaemonia is reliant upon the ability to recognize it. We mustn't confuse the promotive nature of eudaemonia with the idea of "essence." A rock, a stick and fire all have essence, but they have no choice. This is why u is at the bottom of the Philosophy Generator, which has as its species, the constituents of thought itself, the "parts" of paradigm.

It almost seems as if our happiness has taken a back seat to our purpose. Perhaps it has. When we look at the idea of eudaemonia as we've defined it, from within the Philosophy Generator, what can be said? For the sake of clarity and thoroughness, we'll look at even the seemingly redundant positions of u in the PG.

The furthest left, natural experiential norms, we may recall as the necessary associations that make up any part of any particular paradigm. It could be something autonomic, such as humans must hold their breath underwater, or it might be an exemplary tendency, such as we care for our young. These things, as illustrated by the examples I've chosen, may or may not make you happy, but are they promotive? The Philosophy Generator insists that they are eudaemonic ideas by not providing the choice of ~u. To be promotive, an idea such as I must hold my breath underwater, would only be acted upon due to its necessity. Namely, if underwater, I must hold my breath. My degree of happiness in doing so is purely circumstantial, as I'm sure you can well imagine. Am I acting on behalf of the reasons for doing so? Presumably I am, as I am underwater I must. This is the key distinction of the PXN connection. I could jump in the lake and undertake some deep breathing exercises underwater, drowning myself, if I so chose, but if this was the case, I would have to have reasons for doing so. Thus, all naturally occurring experiential norms are eudaemonic. They must be because the reasons for their being are intrinsic. There is no choice, or rather, the choice is made for us.

In the next branch end of the PG we find the u and ~u distinctions of the learned experiential norm. Here we have a complete, reality based, empirical association, either being or having been experienced by the user. In terms of happiness, there is no mystery to the experience. We can simply decide, based on our tangible, biological and mental processes whether or not the association makes us happy or is eudaemonic, but if we wish to make the latter determination, it must be promotive. Unlike the naturally occurring experiential norm, there is a choice to be made. The promotive aspect is revealed by the acceptance of a need for effort and effort made toward the action of choosing. This too is in keeping with my definitions.

Finally, we come to the four boxes, what I have previously referred to as the eudaemonic scale. The first three all have to do with the determination of the ability of a thought to be promotive. Only the last box has to do with the ability to determine happiness. This is why I feel that "promotiveness" outranks happiness in terms of value, importance, goodness and rightness. Also, as the Philosophy Generator makes clear, because the paradigm is being contemplated under the branch of social norms, when we determine something to be eudaemonic under the boxes, we are scoring ourselves on our *ability* to be promotive. Transparency and force of the intention, the evaluability and level of mystery and whether or not it appeals to our logic or emotions all point to the reasons for which we may choose to act or not act eudaemonically. Only our desire to concur or resist, the final box, determines our happiness without being promotive. We may merely react to a paradigm based on this final box, but once we start contemplating why it is we reacted, we have started being promotive and increase eudaemonia. This is the whole point of the PG, to force contemplation, to help you discover eudaemonia, the result of a proper exercising of our essence.

So, it seems our place in life is to *do* what makes us special, reason, rationalize, know and choose. Choosing well, particularly if action is undertook, is the path to virtue and "virtue" is "excellence." (According to Aristotle.) When I look up "virtue" in my dictionary it says, 1.) behaviour showing moral standards, 2.) a good or useful quality of a thing.) When virtue has been achieved through your promotive efforts, it is eudaemonic. However, in Aristotle's Ethics, there are two types of virtues, intellectual and moral. Intellectual virtue is, simply put, the habit of using that big ol' brain of yours, intentionally. Aristotle breaks the intellectual virtues into five categories, which are his attempt to describe what types of thinking we can do: "Science," which is the habit of explaining why something is true. Art, which is the habit of knowing how to make things. Intuition, which is considered a foundation to choosing well, yet is something of a circular definition. (Is it the habit of being in the habit?) I think intuition is something that is in your intentional background. Wisdom, is more properly, "Philos," which means 'love of wisdom.' Wisdom unites the basic principles and is what pushes them, by habit, into intuition. Finally, there is Prudence, which is defined as "acting with or showing care and thought for the future." Being distinguished by the forward thinking directionality of itself, prudence can be described as being promotive, but not the other way around. Prudence is particularly goal specific and deservedly so, in my opinion. All of the intellectual virtues must be in practise in order to be morally virtuous. Ari says it is necessary to know to act rightly, but knowing does not generate right action. Without the intellectual virtues one cannot find the Golden Mean. We must walk before we can dance.

Moral virtue is much more complicated. Where intellectual virtues are the ability to choose and a recognition of the importance of choosing well, moral virtue is taking on an accountability for the choice. It is the habit of choosing the mean of two extremes, in regard to action and emotion. Aristotle calls this "**the Golden Mean**." A mean is akin to "the middle," it is equally distant from two extremes. The two extremes are deficiency and excess. The mean is golden because it is prized. It is not an arbitrary distinction but is a personal opinion, sort of like a sliding scale. Everyone's ideas of deficiency and excess are going to be different. Your ability to discover pleasure in your choices will reflect something of your virtue. (If you feel guilty about a choice, it is because you know it is difficult or wrong.) Sometimes pleasure isn't able to determine morality. There may be instances where we find pleasure in the immoral or interests wane. Sometimes it is not the thing that we find pleasure in that is the problem, but rather *that* we find pleasure in it. The attraction is not to be determined right or wrong, but the *action* is. We shouldn't feel bad about having these feelings, provided we are contemplating what it is we do about them.

Morality itself is a question of what we are either praised for or blamed for. So, questions of morality can only be questions of what we voluntarily do. If we are forced into some action, such as in the case of hyper-manipulation and we choose unpromotively, it isn't really our choosing. Thus, there are factors and modifiers of responsibility. They are, according to Aristotle, knowledge and consent. In order to be fully responsible, we must know what we are doing and consent to it. It is often difficult to determine this knowledge, how much of it is known at the time of choosing, how much *should* we know at the time of choosing, how much of the choosing is due to the habitual background intentionality we all carry around with us. I attempted to answer these concerns with the process that takes place by going through the Philosophy Generator, whereby we attempt to determine how well we are able to think about any given paradigm or intention.

We should take a moment to discuss the idea of

Brian C. Taylor

"voluntary." Aristotle defines the things we "voluntarily do" as "acting according to one's nature," which we certainly could call promotive. So the idea of something being voluntary still may or may not have been contemplated. As in the case of "promotive," "voluntary" does not necessarily indicate eudaemonia. If we are hungry we eat, but if we are sick we may not want to eat. As we know we must eat, we force ourselves to, this is a choice. One does not choose to sneeze, it is involuntary, a reaction and not promotive. However, one is held responsible and accountable for covering that sneeze. Conditions for moral responsibility must be considered for praise or blame, otherwise you are just pitied or excused in some other way, perhaps not because of what you have done, but rather, why you have done it.

In practical terms, there are as many virtues as there are emotions and mental habits. I will publish the list as it is charted by Aristotle, but we could add many, many more. Some of them, we might wish to eliminate from his list. For instance, Ari considers "conversation" to be a virtue. I too would argue that it is, but perhaps this opinion in not shared by you. In terms of excess and deficiency, the conversational scale works from boorishness to buffoonery. Aristotle determines the conversational golden mean to be "wittiness." Perhaps he's right, I'll leave that one up to you to decide. Talk it out amongst yourselves.

My point here is, the list of virtues themselves could be anything. We could consider the virtue of not shouting at sporting events and determine a mean between an excess of team spirit and a lacklustre interest.

We could find the golden mean of the amount of housework, if we so desired.

PARADIGM	EXCESS	MEAN	DEFICIENCY
Fear	Rashness	Courage	Cowardice
Pleasure	Licentiousness	Temperance	Insensibility
Generosity	Prodigality	Liberality	Illiberality
Honour	Vanity	Magnanimity	Pusillanimity
Anger	Irascibility	Patience	Apathy
Expression	Boastfulness	Truthfulness	Understatement
Conduct	Obsequiousness	Friendliness	Cantankerousness
Shame	Shyness	Modesty	Shamelessness

Don't feel bad if you have to get your dictionary, I did. As I've stated, it's not as important to agree with the topics that are divided here. We only need to appreciate what is happening, namely, we establish a mean in whatever concern, by maintaining balance, by aiming for the top of the bell curve, by choosing rightly, from neither extreme. Virtue itself, in spite of whatever you find virtuous, if attached to the idea of the mean, will prevail. The mean cannot steer you wrong. The value of seeking it cannot be overestimated.

Notice how, even in the short list above, we are not being "told what to do." We can, for instance, be angry or cowardly, we just wouldn't want to stay that way for a prolonged length of time. If we did, we would eventually find ourselves coming up short of what would ultimately make us happy. There is a reason that we find our happiness in the mean, it is where we're *supposed* to

Brian C. Taylor

be, nature pushes us there. Contemporaries of Aristotle, a group of Greeks called the Stoics considered him to be wrong in this estimation. The stoics had apathy as a goal, as nearly their entire philosophy. They weren't seeking an abandonment of all feeling, but rather, all reacting. Aristotle said this was impossible, people were always going to get angry and react. Furthermore, he argued, sometimes being angry was the right thing. To seek apathy would be rob us of some of our power. Aristotle sought not to fight our nature, but to embrace it as we do. Like the Stoics, we have efforts to be made, but they needn't be made in vain. One thing both parties agreed on then and we can learn from now, is the importance of habituation. We can only succeed through effort, in everything, always. We can only benefit by practise. Remember, it is what we do that matters. (Doing nothing is still "doing.")

If we make no effort, if we are unable to even comprehend there is an effort to be made, we truly have no hope and Aristotle calls us beasts. He believes there are people on this Earth who can be virtuous without any effort, he calls these people godlike. These would be the Saints of the world. For the rest of, awake, aware and trying, we are broken into two groups: those that struggle and get it right, whom he calls "continent" and those that struggle and get it wrong, whom he calls "incontinent." These two groups make up the bulk of the population, however I contend that the latter, incontinent group is growing. I attribute this growth to the increased complexity and rampant ineptitude displayed by our hyper-manipulated modernity. Many people are in the habit of choosing uneudaemonically, mostly because they aren't aware they're making a choice. These people have no virtue or vice, they have only a struggle. They make the choices they do because they don't even know they have a choice. The ideas of continent and incontinent can be simply expressed as "self-restraint." Either you exercise it or you don't. So we can sum up the idea as "being reactionary is bad." This is yet another reason to develop the habit of contemplation.

As you might have expected, some virtues weigh more heavily on our minds than others. Sometimes you hear of these virtues in your religions, such as there are the four noble truths of the Buddha, the Christian ten commandments, etc. Sometimes they are presented to you where you are employed, perhaps referred to as a mission statement, perhaps listed in a policy manual. There are also different types of virtues as there are different types of "things" in which to find good qualities. We wish to concern ourselves with some of the key virtues that *should be* globally given. As usual, we can expect to find our exemplification of these virtues lacking. Nevertheless, we can only benefit from having this discussion.

Justice is different than other virtues. It is not an emotion, like fear or shame, not a physical sensation like might cause pleasure or pain. When we seek, for instance, courage, we are trying to develop the habit of choosing the mean between being cowardly or rash. The deficiency of cowardice or excessive rashness demonstrates either end of the virtue of courage, but these determinants are responses to fear. Fear is the sphere of feeling from which

Brian C. Taylor

the responses stem. (We are simply calling Aristotle's "sphere of action or feeling," paradigm.) Now we must look at the sphere of action. Justice is simply an idea. Unlike fear, justice is not a response, it is a means to a response in that one might have feelings about it, such as anger or satisfaction, but if you were indifferent to the idea of justice, it wouldn't well up inside you. You have to decide what justice is in a much more active way than deciding what you're afraid of.

Justice is appropriately served, it is fairness, well founded and deserved. Aristotle calls Justice an "action" where the mean is found in balancing reciprocity. Where moral virtue is a habit of choosing the mean as it relates to emotion, justice relates to actions. We would consider one who is able to fairly judge right action as someone who is just. At the same time we are aware we can be pilfered by the usually honest man and helped by a crook. Just as in our moral/emotional sphere, there are degrees of justice. There are also types of justice.

We expect laws to be fair. If they are not, we call them "unjust." They are "unfair." They are unequal. Thus there is a distinction made between lawfulness and equality. This is the difference between "the law demands" and what it "ought to." The distinction between justice and jurisprudence, lawfulness and equality, is the beginning of Natural Law Theory. This philosophy, popularized by the Stoics, states that the Universe is governed by rational principals that we can point to in nature, and as man too was a rational thing, it should be considered natural for us to exercise this law by also being governed by rational principles. So there are natural laws and then there are man-made laws. We, as the subjects of these laws, expect and deserve these laws to be held accountable to what we consider just. The evaluation of equality is our right, as a natural being, able to do so. At least, so says the Natural Law.

Things like murder and stealing we would expect to have legislated, other things, like politeness or other social norms are not, but still get exemplified. As justice is a balancing of giving and taking, these things are no less important, but they are the things that our passions seem not to take advantage of. When we are small children, we learn of fairness by sharing with our siblings or on the playground. If we exhibit any histrionics it is not likely to lead to any new laws being passed.

Aristotle describes different types of Justice as species. The first of which he considers mathematical. He calls it Corrective Justice. Corrective justice is a quantifiable equal exchange. If we are at the market and we buy some bread for a dollar, we could consider this fair. However, if we came the next day to find the same bread for two dollars, we might not want to buy it. This is "voluntary" corrective justice. "This," we say, "is not fair. Justice has not been served here." (A little melodramatic, but not uncommon. We are passionate about our shopping!) Perhaps the vendor will offer two loaves for the same price. This seems like an equal exchange, we are pleased. Both parties have made a mathematical adjustment. In another example of corrective justice, someone steals your car and takes it for a joyride. They crash it and get away unhurt and unpunished. Your car is ruined and you are very displeased indeed. You are down one car and who knows about the thief, he's just gone. There is no justice here, there is only insurance and although having it will replace your vehicle, there is no justice in it. (We want the thief to pay.) Whether purchasing bread or having your car stolen, we seek to have the "giving" and the "taking" to be equal. If it isn't, we desire corrective justice to make it so, mathematically. Note that this distinction is made regardless of who the "giver" and "taker" are.

Our next species of justice is geometrical, as in, there may not be a true equality, in the eyes of different people but there are always reasons available, attached to the idea itself. Aristotle calls this Distributive Justice. Not all things can be measured as equals. These things have to be put in proportional terms. Thus, distinctions are made between the "giver" and the "taker." For instance you might consider it perfectly fair to pay a Doctor more than a Nurse because of more training, or more specialized service. Perhaps you have a dangerous job, it seems to make sense that you would be paid more than someone with the "safe" job. You might live in a country where there is no "death penalty" for murderers, who will probably spend the rest of their lives in jail. You might live in a country where women are stoned to death for adultery. Either of these disciplines are considered just and right by the adjudicators, yet I'm sure you can see how there is a mathematical impurity to them. So geometrical justice is *entirely* relevant to who is doing the judging.

the Authentic Self

So in these two types of justice we have developed schemes. (A plan or way of working toward a goal.) Corrective justice is objective, we are able to quantify what would create equality, mathematically. Distributive justice is subjective and we must think about what would be fair. Using both justices in our lives must be done from within a scheme that is relevant to our circumstances, community, problems faced and not arbitrary. It's not that any scheme will do, we must choose from within our right scheme. Thus, on our planet in 2010, we have murderers living comfortably and adulterers being executed. We should note here that emotions may not correlate with our ideas about justice. We may not like that we have to pay the mechanic seventy-five dollars for twenty minutes work, but we understand that it would have taken us a month to fix the problem because we lack his expertise. (So we understand *why* we must pay him so much.) One has the virtue of being just if one has the habit of choosing the mean between the extremes and giving or taking that which is exactly right, *given the context of the scheme.* If one's feelings are in line with the decision, all the better, but it is not necessary. Aristotle notes that it is in the distributions of justice that the common good is found. He further adds that choosing the right schemes to use is the role of authority. He says, "Politics is the art of the possible." (But let's save this discussion for another day.)

As with all the virtues there must be a method of choosing. Aristotle defines choice as a deliberate desire or a decided want. In terms of our efforts to choose well, in either sphere of emotion or action, we sometimes fail

Brian C. Taylor

to remain neutral. We tend to think of our distributions from within our own points of view and it takes deliberate effort to see all sides. We seek objectivity because we are dealing with action in the real world, not our internal world. Due to the shifting ideas of different people, cultures, movements and time we must work from within quite generalized schemes. Laws, for instance, are generalities. Laws deal with the majority of instances. It is possible for an individual's concerns to have to be determined to be equitable. This is why we have Judges, not only to determine innocence or guilt, not only to sentence fairly, but to determine if the law itself is equitable to the circumstances. This too, we do, in life.

Aristotle, as the father of the syllogism, of which there are sixty-four with sixteen useful, offers us what he calls "the Practical Syllogism." This is the reasoning we do in life, by accident or design, that pushes us into what we are and do. We can state it simply:

A>B
B>C
A>C

The syllogism itself is not that impressive, yet we use it, correctly and incorrectly, all day, every day. It is how we use that illustrates our thinking. The first line is the Universal Premise, this tells us "the rule," what we ought to do. The second line is our desire, it identifies some particular action or an idea we wish to apply. The third line is a non-speculative conclusion. For instance, consider the following scenario: I know lying is wrong. Yet, lying is going to keep me out of jail. So, I'll lie. I might even convince myself to use the lie with other reasoning. I could tell myself that the lie that will keep me out of jail is very clever. As I know very clever things should be said, I can convince myself to tell the lie. (Despite knowing it's wrong.) One can demonstrate this logic by asking someone, (or ourselves,) "What were you thinking?" after having done something morally wrong. We are always rationalizing our actions, it doesn't mean we do so correctly. "Correctly" is a wandering target that goes from impossible to miss to impossible to hit. Note that, although we discuss the thought pattern of the moral wrong-doer, it is always after the fact. The logic is being demonstrated to the world at decision time, whether or not the decision is promotive. This is how Ari knew Socrates was wrong by postulating that one could only be wrong by not knowing. Yes, we are pushed by our passions but it is only by the existence of a paradigm on the subject. The problem here is that all people have their own universal premises, their own ideas about what "ought to be." (As well as not often contemplating them.) Other Philosophers argue this point. They say that as there are wrong choices made without any deliberation, this is proof of evilness in the world. The problem I have with this argument is that it removes the possibility of taking responsibility. (Perhaps this is deliberate.) I see how this interpretation doesn't fit into incontinence as it is not "bad choosing" we are doing, it is "no choosing." We are simply manipulated to certain ends, this we understand. Who or what is doing the manipulating may or may not "be evil" or have intentions that we would consider evil, if we could become aware of them. I'm not saying that "evilness" does not exist, I've listed several

Brian C. Taylor

socially engineered paradigms throughout the book that could be considered evil. I'm saying that the idea of evil itself has a mean that we each walk and even this idea is subject to changing and influential manipulated associations. The idea of what we consider "evil" could be incontinent in and of itself. However, the action demonstrated has to be the product of the bearer, if we are to be authentic. If the evil is within, it must be part of, and if it's part of, there must be, by definition, other parts which we could call "good" parts, from which we may choose. There also might be a lack of any universal premise in the first place. (In which case, we'd probably make one up, being unlikely to leave things well enough alone.) For instance, if I have no inkling as to what one "ought to do," how can I be blamed for not deliberating? What would I deliberate? How could it be called evil that I left something alone, or acted upon being solely driven by my desires? How too is it that I can be blamed when *everyone* exemplifies some particular paradigm and should I refuse, I am subject to ridicule or worse? What if the paradigm is impossible to resist? Some might call this act natural. Luckily for us, this is just an interesting aside.

Justice is one of the four cardinal virtues, along with Prudence, Temperance and Courage. They are called cardinal because Aristotle means them to be a foundation. They are speculative, intellectual virtues that we must have in order to be morally virtuous. Justice, the idea of fairness, can be of some use to us, both intellectually and morally. It is the same with the other three cardinal virtues. Temperance, for instance, means "moderation." Courage itself is the golden mean of our fear paradigm,

the Authentic Self

neither rash, nor cowardly. Prudence, acting or thinking with care for the future, like justice, is a pathway to the mean. One can have a deficiency of prudence or justice, but how can you say one is too just, or too prudent? One can't, so we know that we must reduce these cardinal virtues to their reason for their being, in much the same way that we understand justice to point to the equality that seems to be reflected by natural law.

Courage relates to response to fear. One is considered brave if one feels fear, contemplates the fear and promotively charges on, anyway. This action of contemplation is wholly relevant to our ability to consider the courage of any particular act or thought. If one is not afraid, or is afraid but charges on without knowing why, it is difficult to find courage in the act. Thus, the act of being courageous doesn't point to the act itself, but the ability you have to find the act eudaemonic. Like the idea of justice, we ultimately do the things we do because we seek eudaemonia. It is our pleasure to take part in just acts, to be courageous, to be prudent, to have temperance, indeed, to have all the virtues we can. Without them, we are unhappy, unfulfilled, not using our essence to live up to our purpose. I'm not convinced that courage, while an important virtue, is a cardinal virtue in the same way that Justice is. Courage is helpful because life is challenging, courage also helps one to act and as we know, action is what matters. Justice, however, steers us to "right action." Courage, because of influence, can be summoned just as easily for unjust action. As we already are having problems determining if the judgement we have is sound, if in fact, it is ours at all, introducing the idea of bravely

Brian C. Taylor

charging blindly forward towards these ends seems doubly confounding. Similarly, with the virtue of Temperance, we consider that which we find moderate, in any and all spheres of action or feeling. We can be moderate, in terms of our passions, philosophies and politics. We cannot truly be moderately just. Justice is either on or off. Even if we say, "that's not very fair." We are only saying, "that's not fair."

So I'd like to suggest that there are only two cardinal virtues: Justice and Prudence. They seem to speak to the natural order of things in the universe and are linked to eudaemonia by way being promotive. In fact, because justice and prudence are reliant upon acts of contemplation for their existence, they are causally self referential. This means that we can't help but be virtuous by seeking eudaemonia. If we are doing the thinking, we are doing our job, whether or not we are considered incontinent. The only thing we have to determine our continence is our pleasure response, our determination of "happiness." This is why the concept of happiness must not be removed from the definition of eudaemonia, despite my proposal that it take a back seat to purpose. Sometimes it all comes down to what it is our pleasure to do.

So we must look to the passions that push or pull us, as these emotive beings that we are. Once we find them, we must mentally examine them to create an awareness of which virtues we have to work on. We simply want to be fair and forward thinking. This can be done only through habituation. We must develop the habit of deliberation. I think this habit is lacking in the year

the Authentic Self

2014 as strongly as I feel it must be promoted in order for our continued survival. I don't think we have any choice but to accept the idea of eudaemonia as the standard by which we find pleasure. By introducing the need for a decision or an act to not only please us, but to also be promotive, *as well as* reducing the cardinal virtues to justice and prudence, we will be forced into better thinking. This habituation can be encouraged and internalized into our intentional backgrounds by using the Philosophy Generator to anti-social engineer our paradigms.

Aristotle held that pleasure was natural and could be used to help you live up to your potential. Pleasures, like all things, should seek their mean. All passions are subject for rational choice. It doesn't always work that way, but it is possible for it to work, again given the practice. Passions get brought up in us, in whatever desire you care to name and then we must decide what to do with them. We may just act on them unthinking, which is less than ideal, but as we are capable of deliberation, we are *supposed* to be in control. We have the ability to choose the right path, the onus is on us to do so and do so wisely. Ari thinks pleasure is associated with bodily and mental activities, but as it can be derived from a mere decision, pleasure is part of the activity, it is not the goal. Pleasure and/or happiness is not the be all and end all of ethics, but it can point to where virtue might reside, or be lacking. So it seems that Aristotle agrees that happiness should take a back seat to essence, yet not be ignored. It is a wind we can steer into.

Furthermore, the things that we take pleasure in,

Brian C. Taylor

can and will change, via the process of maturing, through circumstance, by effort. Pleasure can come from choosing rightly on the mean. Stopping bad habits, encouraging good ones. We all seek happiness, whatever that means, but all creatures do so, from within what abilities they have. A whale seeks his happiness as much as a slug, it doesn't make it eudaemonia. It seems only we humans have the option of consciously working our happiness. We know the path to the happiness we seek is in the contemplative nature of seeking virtue. Real necessities should not be the concern of our happiness, these things are non-negotiable. You're not going to choose to freeze or starve. Happiness comes from choosing rightly. If we go too far, or have too much of a good thing, it is inevitable and natural that an end shall be forced.

~   ~   ~

In terms of the overall theme of this book, I see the eudaemonic deficiency of the human population as a manifestation of two possible phenomenon: Either we seek mere happiness instead of eudaemonia, or we seek what we think is eudaemonic, but is not. By seeking only shallow happiness we are responding to our needs, which may or may not be virtuous. Without being promotive there is no chance for eudaemonia and every chance for deficiency or excess. In fact, it is in all likelihood that the ultimate unhappiness you can come to know will force the promotive nature and convince you to change. (How sad it is that you didn't just think about it in the first place.) Perhaps this is a major part of the problem, seeking incomplete happiness.

In the second manifestation of the eudaemonic

the Authentic Self

deficiency of modernity, we become mistakenly convinced of eudaemonism. Obviously, as we have made a choice, albeit an incontinent one, we are being promotive. We are acting on behalf of the reasons for doing so, which implies that we are aware of them. However, it is possible to be *wrong about them.* Perhaps this represents a much larger portion of our ideas about happiness. We can be made happy by some rather strange things. This is where time comes into our factoring.

When we find ourselves caring about something or harming something, it is because we feel a certain way. However, when we are hyper-manipulated to feel a certain way about something, we may come to realize a very tangible internal conflict about the paradigm. This is especially true if we act on the intention to discover "inappropriate" emotions. For instance, your army isn't going to perform well if it's squeamish about killing people and your family isn't going to perform very well if you don't care for them. In both of these examples, it is *your* intentionality that matters, however, by definition, if we are hyper-manipulated, our say in the matter is diminished, if not completely absent. This is why your authentic thoughts on any socially engineered paradigm can only be exposed by either contemplation, or time. If you're unwilling or unable to do the thinking required, your determination of happiness will, via time, eventually bring you to a determination of either virtue or vice. The universe demands balance, but you have the ability to balance yourself.

Visit anti-socialengineering.com for more information.

Brian C. Taylor

the Authentic Self

www.ingramcontent.com/pod-product-compliance
Lightning Source LLC
Chambersburg PA
CBHW060430290526
45791CB00002B/919